The Singer's Manual of German and French Diction

by Dr. Richard G. Cox

Faculty, University of North Carolina School of Music

SCHIRMER BOOKS
A Division of Macmillan Publishing Co., Inc.
NEW YORK

COLLIER MACMILLAN PUBLISHERS
LONDON

Copyright © 1970 by Schirmer Books
A Division of Macmillan Publishing Co., Inc.

SCHIRMER BOOKS
A Division of Macmillan Publishing Co., Inc.
866 Third Avenue, New York, N.Y. 10022

Collier Macmillan Canada, Ltd.

Library of Congress Catalog Card Number: 78-113926

Printed in the United States of America

printing number
9   10

CONTENTS

Introduction

The purpose of this manual is to provide a concise guide to the pronunciation of German and French as applied to the performance of vocal literature in these languages. The procedure followed here will be the presentation of the language sounds as represented by the alphabet of the International Phonetic Association (IPA), showing the correspondence of these sounds and the spelling of these sounds in the respective languages, followed by an alphabetic summary showing the same correspondence from the opposite direction. The IPA alphabet is used because these symbols represent specific sounds which remain constant for all languages and therefore are considerably more precise than such statements as "The French *é* is pronounced like the long *a* in English." It must be fully understood, however, that these symbols, unlike the letters of any specific language, represent the same sound whenever they are used. In order to remove any possibility of confusion between these symbols and actual alphabet letters, phonetic symbols are customarily placed within square brackets.

Whenever feasible throughout the text that follows, every effort will be made to identify the sound represented by the symbols in terms of the English usage of the sound and to indicate what differences, if any, exist between the pronunciation of the symbol in English and the pronunciation of the same symbol in German or French.[1] Nevertheless, it is obviously impossible to define a sound so narrowly in writing that anyone but an experienced phonetician can pronounce it without having heard it. It is therefore most strongly recommended that some oral and listening work be done as a supplement to the use of this manual. Recordings by native-speaking singers in the two languages are indispensable, not so much from the standpoint of imitating the pronunciation of specific pieces as from that of acquiring an ear for the sounds that are peculiar to the two languages. Since the diction of baritones—because of the range in which they sing—is often the easiest to apprehend, recordings by Dietrich Fischer-Dieskau and

---

[1] For further study of the phonetic alphabet as it applies to English, see also Marshall, *The Singer's Manual of English Diction* (New York: G. Schirmer, 1946), p. 123f; Kenyon, *American Pronunciation* (Ann Arbor: George Wahr Publishing Company, 1950), p. 24f. A comprehensive examination of the comparison between English and German pronunciation may be found in William G. Moulton's *The Sounds of English and German* (Chicago: University of Chicago Press, 1962).

Gérard Souzay are especially recommended, not only for the supreme technical and artistic heights attained by these two great singers but also for the beauty, precision and intelligibility of their diction. It is also recommended that students of diction in these languages work with tape recorders so as to hear their own efforts more accurately. For this purpose, the words and song excerpts given to illustrate each sound as it is presented might be useful. Appendix III is a series of exercises in "adjacent vowel sounds" in French, which should be useful for oral work. In these lists each of three words is identical in pronunciation except for a slight adjustment of the vowel.

As a final supplement to the use of this manual, it is recommended that the student practice making phonetic transcriptions of material in the languages that he is studying; that is, write out a full representation of the sounds in phonetic symbols. Appendices II and IV include transcriptions of a few familiar examples; the student is advised to transcribe the pieces for himself and then compare what he has done with the printed material. Further comparisons may be found in *Phonetic Readings of Songs and Arias.*[2]

As an introduction to the phonetic symbols to be used throughout this manual, Figures 1 and 2 show the consonants and the vowels in their orderly phonetic arrangements. All consonants are formed by bringing some part of the lower mouth into some relation with some part of the upper mouth. Consonants are classified in three ways (see Figure 1). First, they are classified according to the nature of the relationship between the two parts of the mouth. Thus, a "stop" is a consonant formed by bringing the two parts of the mouth absolutely together to prevent the passage of air between them. A "nasal" is a consonant formed in the same way but with air passing through the nose. A "fricative" is a consonant formed by bringing the two parts of the mouth just close enough together to cause a sound of friction to result when air passes between them. An "affricate" is a combination of a stop and a fricative pronounced in the same place in the mouth. A "glide" is a vowel shortened so much as to sound like a consonant. The term "liquid" is a convenient designation for the consonants [l] and [r] but does not, like the other terms, reveal any information about the formation of these consonants.

Second, consonants may be classified according to the part of the mouth involved in their articulation. Thus, a consonant articulated by the two lips is called "labial"; a consonant involving the lower lip and the

---

[2] Berton Coffin *et al., Phonetic Readings of Songs and Arias* (Boulder: Pruett Press, 1964). The student of French diction should be warned that in one or two details, especially in the use of *liaison,* the French transcriptions are geared more toward conversational French than toward the usual pronunciation of French singers of opera and *mélodie.* Nevertheless, 'this is an excellent reference work for the student of diction. No singer, of course, has mastered these languages until he can make such transcriptions for himself.

	Labial	Labio-dental	Alveolar	Alveolo-palatal	Palatal	Velar	Glottal
Stops							
voiced	b		d			g	
voiceless	p		t			k	* ʔ
Nasals							
voiced	m		n		† ɲ	* ŋ	
Fricatives							
voiced		v	z	† ʒ	* j		
voiceless		f	s	ʃ	* ç	* x	* h
Affricates							
voiceless		* pf	* ts				
Liquids			l				
			r				
Glides	† w				† j		
					† ɥ		

* Used only in German.
† Used only in French.

FIGURE 1

Systematic Arrangement of Consonants

upper teeth is designated "labio-dental." Since the ridge of gum behind the upper teeth is called the "alveolar ridge," an "alveolar" consonant is one articulated by the blade of the tongue against the gum ridge, and an "alveolo-palatal" consonant is one formed slightly farther back toward the hard palate. A consonant involving the top of the tongue and the hard palate is termed "palatal," and one articulated by the back of the tongue and the soft palate, or velum, is called "velar."

Finally, consonants may be classified as "voiced" or "voiceless" according to whether the vocal cords are in vibration or not. Voiceless consonants are those that may be whispered; voiced consonants require vibration of the vocal cords for full clarity.

Since all the signs used in the diagrams are phonetic symbols, the customary brackets are omitted. Instead, an asterisk is used to indicate symbols found only in German and a dagger to show symbols used only in French.

The usual representation of vowels is in a diagram (see Figure 2) the top of which represents the roof of the mouth and the bottom the lowest possible angle of the jaw. The left side represents the front of the mouth, the right side the back of the mouth. All this has to do primarily with the position of the tongue. Thus, the tongue is nearest the roof of the mouth for the "high" vowels and nearest the lowered jaw for the "low" vowels. The point at which the tongue approaches the roof of the mouth is farther forward for the "front" vowels, and farther back for the "back" vowels. However, singers must, of course, exercise every caution against moving most of the tongue back for the "back" vowels, since nothing is more detrimental to a clear singing tone. This can be done easily by using the middle of the tongue to approach the roof of the mouth for the front vowels, and the back of the tongue for the back vowels. In this diagram, though nowhere else in this manual, a symbol placed in parentheses is the conventional indication of lip-rounding.

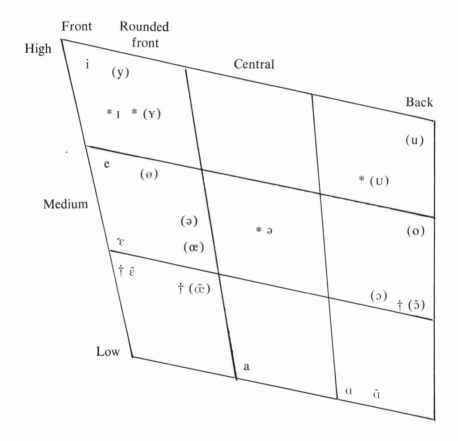

FIGURE 2
Vowel Diagram

Figure 3 is a summary of the phonetic alphabet in the order in which the symbols will be presented in each chapter of this book, showing sample words for the approximate use of the sound, if any, in English.

VOWELS

A. Front Vowels	B. Rounded Front Vowels	C. Back Vowels	D. The Neutral Vowel	E. Nasal Vowels
[i] *see*	[y] NONE	[u] *noon*	[ə] (German) *the*	[ɛ̃] *can't*
[ɪ] *sit*	[ʏ] NONE	[ʊ] *book*		[ɑ̃] *pomp*
[e] *chaotic*	[ø] NONE	[o] *obey*		[ɔ̃] *gaunt*
[ɛ] *set*	[œ] NONE	[ɔ] *all*		[œ̃] NONE
[a] h*a*lf (New England)	[ə] (French) NONE	[ɑ] *calm*		

CONSONANTS

A. Stops	B. Nasals	C. Fricatives	D. Affricates	E. Glides	F. Liquids
[b] *baby*	[m] *murmur*	[v] *verve*	[pf] camp*f*ire	[ɪ] (German) *yes*	[l] *lily*
[p] *paper*	[n] *noon*	[f] *fife*	[ts] hi*ts*	[j] (French)	[r] *very*
[d] *did*	[ɲ] *onion*	[z] *mazes*		[ɥ] NONE	
[t] *title*	[ŋ] *singing*	[s] *recess*		[w] *word*	
[g] *gag*		[ʒ] *vision*			
[k] *kick*		[ʃ] *hush*			
		[j] *yes* (very emphatic)			
		[ç] NONE			
		[x] NONE			
		[h] *haphazard*			

FIGURE 3

Summary of the Phonetic Alphabet

There are three modifications of phonetic symbols which will not be used in this manual but which the reader may wish to know about. In phonetic transcript primary stress is indicated by placing a mark above the beginning of a syllable, secondary stress by placing a mark below the beginning of a syllable. For example, the English verb *compliment* would be transcribed ['kɑmplɪ‚mɛnt]. Vowel length (or occasionally consonant length) is shown by placing a colon after the symbol. The English word *dawn* can thus be distinguished from the French word *donne* by transcribing the former [dɔːn] and the latter [dɔn]. Neither of these modifications will be used here because the singer will normally take his cues for both stress and vowel length from the composer. A third possible modification is the placing of an asterisk before the ́ beginning of a proper name in phonetic transcript, since phonetic symbols are never capitalized. Thus the name *John* is transcribed [*dʒɑn]. While this facilitates the reading of an extended passage in phonetic transcript, it contributes nothing to the kind of use we will make of phonetic symbols.

Let it be remembered that this is an introduction to the study of phonetics. Therefore, in the survey of French presented here, many exceptional usages have been omitted in the interest of clarity; an attempt has been made, however, to include such exceptional usages as are commonly found in vocal literature. The advanced student of French is referred to the works on French diction listed in the bibliography.

Chapter I

GERMAN VOWELS [1]

I. GERMAN VOWELS IN REVIEW

Most German vowels may be paired according to spelling and are distinguished by the fact that one of the pair is closed, the other open. Furthermore, closed vowels are always long except in unstressed syllables; and open vowels, except *ä*, are always short. The following chart illustrates this:

Spelling	Closed Pronunciation	Open Pronunciation
i	[i]	[ɪ]
e	[e]	[ɛ]
o	[o]	[ɔ]
u	[u]	[ʊ]
ü, y	[y]	[ʏ]
ö	[ø]	[œ]

Since most vowels occur in these pairs, a very useful way to introduce German vowels is to review the distinctions between closed vowels on the one hand and open vowels on the other.

A. CLOSED VOWELS OCCUR IN THESE POSITIONS:

1. Final: Alibi, Ade, jetzo, du.
2. Double: Meer, Boot.
3. Before *h* in the same syllable (see Chapter II, section C-9): ihnen, Ehre, wohnen, Ruhe, Möhre, Bühne.
4. Before a single consonant followed by a vowel: wider, leben, kosen, Muse, Düne, hören.

[1] There is a wide variety of pronunciations of German current throughout German-speaking countries. The present discussion follows the principles of the so-called *Bühnenaussprache*, the pronunciation which is accepted on the stage throughout Germany today. An excellent treatment of the varieties of German speech may be found in pp. 1–6 of Viëtor's *German Pronunciation: Practice and Theory*, 5th edition (Leipzig: O. R. Reisland, 1913).

Exceptions:

a. *e* in an unstressed syllable is often [ə] (see Chapter I, Part II, section D).

b. *i* is open in inflections of the suffix *ig:* ewiger, selige.

c. The open vowel in the prefixes *er, her, hin, in, mit, ob, um, un, ver, von* and *zer* remains open when the prefix is followed directly by a vowel.

5. Usually before a single final consonant in a monosyllable or in a stressed final syllable: Medizin, Weg, schon, schön, für, nun, zum.

6. Before the following combined consonants:

a. Before *ch, u* is usually [u], *o* is sometimes [o]: Buch, suchen, sucht, hoch.

b. Before ss (ß), *o, u* and *ü* are sometimes closed: gross, Fuss, süss; however, *i* and *e* are always open, and occasionally *o, u* and *ü.*

7. Occasionally before two or more consonants.

a. When the consonant cluster is the result of an inflective ending of some kind, the vowel quality of the stem or root form of the word is retained, even though the vowel itself may change.

(1) Verb inflections: *lebst* (from leben), *hört* (from hören), *lobt* (from loben), *rufst* (from rufen), *gibt* (from geben).

(2) Diminutive endings: *Röslein* (from *Rose*), *Füsschen* (from *Fuss*).

(3) Noun endings: *Botschaft* (from *Bote*), *Schönheit* (from *schön*).

(4) Adjective endings: *schönste* (from *schön*), *gütlich* (from *Güte*).

b. When the consonant cluster happens as a result of the compounding of two words, the first of which normally has a closed vowel before the final consonant: *rotblühenden.*

c. *e* is closed before *r* followed by other consonants in a few common words: Erde, werden, erst, Pferd, Werth, Schwert.

d. *o* is irregularly closed in *Mond* and *Trost.*

B. OPEN VOWELS OCCUR IN THESE POSITIONS:

1. Before two or more consonants: immer, endlich, offnen, Mord, dunkel, hübsch.

Exceptions: see section 7 above.

2. Occasionally before a single final consonant in a monosyllable: ob, im, um, vom, bin, hin, in, von, bis, des, es, mit, weg (as an adverb; not *Weg* as a noun), and in compounds of such words as *herum, wohin, damit,* etc.

3. Before the following combinations of consonants representing a single sound:

a. Before *ch, i* and *e* are always open: ich, sprechen; *o* is sometimes open: doch, noch.
b. Before *ck,* all vowels are open: Blicke, decken, Glück, Ruck, Stock.
c. Before *ng* all vowels are open: singen, eng, Rechnung, Jünger.
d. Before ss (ß), *i* and *e* are always open: hissen, essen; *o, u* and *ü* are sometimes open: Fluss, küssen, Ross.
e. Before *sch:* Tisch, Esche, Busch, Büsche.

II. GERMAN VOWELS IN DETAIL

A. FRONT VOWELS

1. [i]
   a. *Description* This is the highest and most forward of the vowels, as can be seen from reviewing the Vowel Diagram, Figure 2. Its pronunciation corresponds to that of the "long *e*" in English, except that the tongue is less relaxed than in English, especially as pronounced in the United States.
   b. *German spellings*
   i in closed position: Alibi, ihm, mir.
   ie: sie, vielleicht.
   Exception: In unstressed syllables of many words of Latin derivation, especially proper names, names of flowers and plants, and words denoting nationality, *ie* is pronounced [ĭə]: Familie, Lilie, Spanien.
   ieh: Vieh.
   c. *Examples from vocal literature*
   Du bist vom Himmel m*i*r besch*ie*den.
   (*Widmung;* Rückert, Schumann)
   Ich will *ih*m d*ie*nen, *ih*m leben.
   (*Der Ring;* Chamisso, Schumann)
   L*ie*ber bleib ich h*ie*r, lächelt Laura m*i*r.
   (*Seligkeit;* Hölty, Schubert)

2. [ɪ]
   a. *Description* Note that on the vowel diagram this vowel is only slightly lower than [i] but it is articulated with the tongue even more retracted than for [e], the next lower vowel. This is the vowel used for the "short *i*" in English. Again, singers should be cautioned against a tongue-position which is too much retracted and relaxed, as is often the case in American speech.
   b. *Spellings*
   i in open position: immer, singen, ewiglich, mit, hin.
   i in the suffixes *ig, in* and *nis:* selig, Müllerin, Geheimnis.

c. *Examples from vocal literature*
Mein Herz still in sich singet.

(*Intermezzo;* Eichendorff, Schumann)

Ich finde sie nimmer und nimmermehr.

(*Gretchen am Spinnrade;* Goethe, Schubert)

Wohin, sprich, wohin?

(*Wohin;* Müller, Schubert)

3. [e]

a. *Description*   This is a vowel which does not normally exist in
pure form in English except in short, unstressed syllables like the
first syllable of *chaotic* or *fatality*. Most English-speaking people
use an off-glide toward [ɪ] when the "long *a*" vowel occurs in a
long, stressed syllable (may, late, vain). Exceptions may be
found in the Scottish and Irish dialects and in much of the speech
of the American western-plains states, where a true [e] may be
heard in stressed syllables. Singers should studiously avoid the
customary off-glide when pronouncing this vowel in German and
should carefully practice the distinction between [e] and [ɛ], a
distinction which is very much in evidence in the diction of native
German singers. Note that on the vowel diagram this vowel has
a more forward tongue position than [ɪ]. It is very close in sound
to [i]—in fact, so close that one may sometimes mistake it for
[i] in listening to German singers, who always pronounce it more
like [i] than like [ɛ].

b. *Spelling*
e in closed position: je, Meer, Kehle, den, Leder, lebst.

c. *Examples from vocal literature*
Du meine Welt, in der ich lebe.

(*Widmung;* Rückert, Schumann)

Da hast du mich erst belehrt.

(*Der Ring;* Chamisso, Schumann)

Dem Schnee, dem Regen, dem Wind entgegen.

(*Rastlose Liebe;* Goethe, Schubert)

Wenn sie entschwebt dem Thal der Erden.

(*Tannhäuser;* Wagner)

4. [ɛ]

a. *Description*   This is very much the sound of the "short *e*" in
English (met, head, friend) but is, of course, the clipped, pure
"short *e*" of British English and not the frequently prolonged and
diphthongized "short *e*" heard in the southern United States.

b. *Spellings*
e in open position: denn, beste, brechen, des, es.

ä, which is lengthened to [ɛː] in "closed position" but is always
pronounced with open quality:

älter, Männer (short).
Mähr, Mädel (long).
c. *Examples from vocal literature*
Hell und herrlich jener Stern.
                    (*Er, der Herrlichste;* Chamisso, Schumann)
Es zog eine Hochzeit den Berg entlang.
                    (*Im Walde;* Eichendorff, Schumann)
Schweigt, ihr versteckten Gesänge.
                    (*Ruhe, Süssliebchen;* Tieck, Brahms)
Engeln und Verklärten.
                    (*Seligkeit;* Hölty, Schubert)

B. ROUNDED FRONT VOWELS

The rounded front vowels are pronounced exactly like the corresponding front vowels, except that the lips are rounded. Mastery of these is perfectly simple once this principle is firmly established. It is also most important to take care to round the lips before the preceding consonant is completed. Delay in rounding the lips results in a most un-German-sounding diphthong.

1. [y]
   a. *Description*   This vowel has the tongue-position of [i] combined with the lip-position of [u].
   b. *Spellings*
      ü in closed position: kühl, für, über.
      y in closed position: Asyl, Zypresse.
   c. *Examples from vocal literature*
      Sie blüht und glüht und leuchtet.
                    (*Die Lotosblume;* Heine, Schumann)
      Frisch grünendem Hügel und Frühlingsblüten.
                    (*An eine Aeolsharfe;* Mörike, Brahms)
      Will suchen einen Zypressenhain,
      Eine Heide voll grünen Rosmarein.
                    (*Die liebe Farbe;* Müller, Schubert)

2. [Y]
   a. *Description*   [Y] is rather difficult to pronounce, since it combines the tongue-position of [ɪ] with the lip-position of [ʊ]. Singers should practice approaching [y] and [Y] from [i] and [ɪ] respectively, being careful to make no change between them except the rounding of the lips.
   b. *Spellings*
      ü in open position: hübsch, künftig.
      y in open position: Myrthe.
   c. *Examples from vocal literature*
      Sei mir gegrüsst, sei mir geküsst!
                    (*Sei mir gegrüsst;* Rückert, Schubert)

O w*ü*sst ich doch den Weg zur*ü*ck.

(*O wüsst ich doch;* Groth, Brahms)

Laue L*ü*fte, Blumend*ü*fte.

(*Lob der Thränen;* Schlegel, Schubert)

3. [ø]

   a. *Description*   [ø] combines the tongue-position of [e] with lip-rounding almost as tense as that for [y]. The difficulty that most non-German singers have with this vowel can easily be remedied by establishing the correct tongue-position for [e]. Because the sound of the vowel [ø] and that of the following vowel [œ] superficially resemble that of the English vowel [ɜ], which is always spelled with an *r* (her, murmur, bird, word, learn), English-speaking singers occasionally allow an "r-color" to intrude upon these German vowels. Nothing could sound less convincing as an attempt to pronounce a German sound. The striking difference between [ø] and [œ] on the one hand and [ɜ] on the other is that the two German vowels are pronounced with lip-rounding, whereas the English vowel is not.

   b. *Spelling*

   ö (*oe*) in closed position: böse, Höh, Goethe.

   c. *Examples from vocal literature*

Ich hörte die V*ö*gel schlagen.

(*Im Walde;* Eichendorff, Schumann)

Diese Wolken in den H*ö*hen, dieser V*ö*glein munt'rer Zug.

(*An die ferne Geliebte;* Jeitelles, Beethoven)

4. [œ]

   a. *Description*   This vowel has the tongue-position for [ɛ] with lips that are round but much more relaxed and open than with any of the preceding vowels.

   b. *Spelling*

   ö (*oe*) in open position: öffnen, Götter, löschen.

   c. *Examples from vocal literature*

Jauchzen M*ö*cht' ich, m*ö*chte weinen.

(*Frühlingsnacht;* Eichendorff, Schumann)

Weit ge*ö*ffnet lacht sein Aug.

(*Die Walküre;* Wagner)

C. BACK VOWELS

The back vowels are all rounded in German and should, as previously noted, be carefully rounded before the end of the preceding consonant. Failure to round the lips at all will produce the flat sound that these vowels are often given in the southern United States; delay in rounding the lips will result in a diphthong instead of a pure vowel.

1. [u]

   a. *Description*   [u] is the highest back vowel. This is the sound of *oo* in such English words as *cool* and *noon,* but somewhat tenser in tongue-position and in lip-rounding. It is not the sound of the *u* in such English words as *fury* and *music,* which begins in an unrounded glide.

b. *Spelling*

u in closed position: du, Kuh, nun, Fuss, Buch, Pudel, Zum.

c. *Examples from vocal literature*

D*u* bist die R*u*h.

(*Du bist die Ruh;* Rückert, Schubert)

N*u*r in Dem*u*th ihn betrachten.

(*Er, der Herrlichste;* Chamisso, Schumann)

Die müden Augen z*u*z*u*t*u*n.

(*O wüsst ich doch;* Groth, Brahms)

2. [u]

a. *Description* [u] has the same relation to [u] as [ɪ] to [i]. The tongue is lower but also farther forward in its approach to the palate. Again, the very relaxed, neutral and unrounded sound this vowel often acquires in English speech (book, could, put) is to be carefully avoided.

b. *Spelling*

u in open position: Fluss, Mund, brunnen, um.

c. *Examples from vocal literature*

*U*nd s*u*mmen zum Schl*u*mmer dich ein.

(*Ruhe, Süssliebchen;* Tieck, Brahms)

Sein Händedr*u*ck, *u*nd ach, sein K*u*ss!

(*Gretchen am Spinnrade;* Goethe, Schubert)

3. [o]

a. *Description* This sound, like [e], is seldom found in pure form in an English stressed syllable, where it usually acquires an off-glide toward [u] (go, moan, hold). Like [e] it is sometimes found in unstressed syllables (*o*bey, foll*o*w); and the speech of the same areas where [e] is heard in stressed syllables will often employ [o] in stressed syllables as well. Again, the off-glide that usually characterizes this sound in English should be rigorously avoided in German. Also to be avoided is the delay in rounding the lips that often distorts this vowel, especially in British English.

b. *Spelling*

o in closed position: so, Mozart, hoch, Pohl, Boot, Mond.

c. *Examples from vocal literature*

Es z*o*g eine H*o*chzeit den Berg entlang.

(*Im Walde;* Eichendorff, Schumann)

*O*hne sie ist alles t*o*t.

(*Minnelied;* Hölty, Brahms)

W*o* die R*o*se hier blüht.

(*Anakreons Grab;* Goethe, Wolf)

4. [ɔ]

   a. *Description*   This vowel is lower and less round than [o]. It is the vowel sound often spelled in English with *au, aw* or *a* before *l* (autumn, law, tall), except that whereas this vowel is always long in English, it is always short in German. Like the distinction between [e] and [ɛ], that between [o] and [ɔ] is most important to acceptable German diction and can be heard very clearly in the pronunciation of native German singers. English-speaking singers should avoid confusing this vowel with the "short o" of English, which is of course not an "o" vowel at all but a short (and sometimes slightly rounded) form of "ah." Also to be avoided is the unrounding of this vowel to the English vowel [ʌ], as in *mud, love, tough.*

   b. *Spelling*
   o in open position: voll, Zorn, ob, von.

   c. *Examples from vocal literature*
   Der Hut flog mir vom Kopfe.
                       (*Der Lindenbaum;* Müller, Schubert)
   Die Sonne hebt sich noch einmal.
                        (*Die Stadt;* Heine, Schubert)
   Es rollet der Donner.
                  (*Die junge Nonne;* Craigher, Schubert)

5. [a]

   a. *Description*   The German *a* may be pronounced short or long according to the rules given for open and closed vowels in the first part of this chapter.[2] In general, even when it is long, it is not so dark a vowel as that in the English words *calm* and *father.* When it is short, it is not the English "short o" (*stop, not,* except as sometimes pronounced in the western United States) but a short form of the vowel used in Great Britain and New England in such words as *half, path, ask.*

   b. *Spellings*
   a, aa, ah: als, Mann, Paar, fahren.

   c. *Examples from vocal literature*
   O liebliche Wangen, ihr macht mir verlangen.
              (*O liebliche Wangen;* Flemming, Brahms)
   Ich sah sie fallen auf deine Hand.
                      (*Am Meer;* Heine, Schubert)
   Dass sie wachsen, dass sie blühen.
              (*Träume;* Wesendonck, Wagner)

---

[2] Moulton, *op. cit.,* p. 62, makes a good case for qualitative as well as quantitative distinction between the two sounds of *a* in German speech. Most authorities, however, distinguish the two only by length; and any differences in quality—as Marshall points out in connection with the "broad *a*" and the "half-broad *a*" of English, *op. cit.,* p. 163—are likely, anyway, to be less prominent in singing than in speech.

D. THE NEUTRAL VOWEL. [ə]

1. *Description*
   The neutral or "schwa" vowel is used very often in German, though less so in song than in speech. The sound of this vowel is the neutral, open sound found in many English unstressed syllables (the, upon, along, government). However, just as in English we often restore [ə] to a full vowel sound in singing because of the pitch, duration or metric position of the note to be sung on it; so in German, native singers often sing [ɛ] for the same reason. This is less common with the final e or er than with the other combinations which employ the schwa in German speech. Note also that the German pronunciation of the schwa has more tension, and tends to be rounder and more forward than its English counterpart.

2. *Spellings*   e in the following positions:
   a. In the prefixes *ge* and *be:* geboren, bedenken.
   b. Final in an unstressed syllable: Liebe, grosse.
   c. Before *l, ln, lnd, lst, lt, m, n, nd, ns, r, rs, rst, rt, s, st* and *t* in final unstressed syllables: Nebel, lispeln, lispelnd, lispelst, lispelt, diesem, singen, singend, Mutter, Vaters, Lebens, dauerst, dauert, gutes, ruhest, kehret.
   d. Before the same consonants and consonant clusters in unstressed syllables followed by inflective endings: liebende, andere, Schwesterlein.
   e. In compound words where the first part of the compound ends in unstressed *e,* or in unstressed *e* followed by one of the consonants or consonant clusters listed under (c): Maienglokken, tausendmal, Tugendgefühle (note the presence of the [ə] not only in the second but also in the third syllable, since *ge* is the prefix to the second part of the compound), Wonnevoll.

3. *Examples from vocal literature*
   Lied erschalle, feiernd walle mein Gebet zur Himmelshalle!

   (*Der Freischütz;* Weber)

   Mitten in Schimmer der spiegelnden Wellen.

   (*Auf dem Wasser zu singen;* Stolberg, Schubert)

E. DIPHTHONGS

German diphthongs are all "falling"; that is, all have the primary stress on the first vowel. Therefore they should be sung with the longer part of the note-value on the first vowel. The second element of the diphthong, however, is more prominent in German than in English, and care must be taken to sound the second element quite distinctly. A deft, sharp motion of the tongue, or of the tongue and lips together, is required to make the second element clearly articulate but very short.

1. [ae]
   a. *Description*   This diphthong has a superficial resemblance to the diphthong in the English words *my, fine, eye,* which is represented phonetically [aɪ] with the tongue more relaxed and farther back for the second element than for the [ae] in German.
   b. *Spellings*
      ai: Hain, Mai.   *ay:* Bayreuth.
      ei: Geist, Meister.   *ey:* Meyer.
   c. *Examples from vocal literature*
      Nur *ei*ne Mutter w*ei*ss all*ei*n.

      (*An meinem Herzen;* Chamisso, Schumann)
      Es brennt m*ei*n *Ei*ngew*ei*de.

      (*Lied der Mignon;* Goethe, Schubert)
      Und r*ei*cher blüht und r*ei*cher glänzt der M*ai*.

      (*Wie sollten wir geheim sie halten;* Schack, Strauss)
2. [ao]
   a. *Description*   This is somewhat like the diphthong in the English words *now, house,* which, however, is represented phonetically [aʊ], with the lips less round and the tongue farther forward than for the German [ao].
   b. *Spelling*
      au: Bauer, Frau, Haus.
   c. *Examples from vocal literature*
      O *A*ugen, so s*au*gen das Licht meiner *A*ugen.

      (*O liebliche Wangen;* Flemming, Brahms)
      R*au*schender Strom, br*au*sender Wald.

      (*Aufenthalt;* Rellstab, Schubert)
3. [ɔø]
   a. *Description*   This is superficially similar to the diphthong in the English words *boy, voice,* which is represented phonetically [ɔɪ] with the lips unrounded and the tongue more relaxed for the second element than for that of the German diphthong [ɔø].
   b. *Spellings*
      äu: Fräulein, Tannhäuser.
      eu: Freude, heute.
   c. *Examples from vocal literature*
      Sag, welch wunderbare Tr*äu*me . . . dass sie nicht wie leere Sch*äu*me.

      (*Träume;* Wesendonck, Wagner)
      Wenn die f*eu*chten Augen l*eu*chten.

      (*Lob der Thränen;* Schlegel, Schubert)

Chapter II

GERMAN CONSONANTS

A. STOPS

Like English, German uses six stops: [b], [p], [d], [t], [g] and [k]. Before describing each one in detail, it is necessary to set forth one preliminary rule: a stop coming at the end of a word is always voiceless. In addition, a stop preceding another consonant is voiceless except in cases where *bl, br, dr, gl, gn* or *gr* occurs in the same syllable. (These combinations are always in the same syllable when they occur together unless the first consonant is part of a prefix, as in *abreisen;* the end of a stem preceding a suffix, as in *farblos;* or the end of the first part of a compound word, as in *Zugluft.*) Also, stops are voiceless in final consonant clusters, as in *hübsch, liegt, Stadt.* Finally, a stop may become voiceless before a vowel if the stop is the end of a prefix (A*b*art) or if it is the first part of a compound word (lie*b*entflammten) and is therefore separated syllabically from the vowel.

1. [b]
   a. *Description* [b] is the voiced labial stop and corresponds exactly to the English pronunciation of *b*.
   b. *Spellings*
      b except at the end of a word or syllable: Bern, bringen, Anblick, aber.
      bb: Ebbe.[1]
   c. *Examples from vocal literature*
      Ich *b*licke *b*is zum Grund.

      (*Dein blaues Auge;* Groth, Brahms)
      Was im *B*usen ich *b*arg, was ich *b*in.

      (*Die Walküre;* Wagner)
2. [p]
   a. *Description* [p] is the voiceless labial stop, corresponding to the English pronunciation of the letter *p*.

---

[1] Except for *s*, which becomes voiceless between vowels, doubled consonants in German are pronounced phonetically like single ones. However, there should be a slight lingering on the sound so that the doubled consonant sounds doubled and so that the preceding vowel is slightly shortened.

17

b. *Spellings*

p, pp: Papier, Puppe, Preis.

b at the end of a word: Stab, ob.

b at the end of a syllable: Ablaut, lieblich,[2] obgleich.

b in a final combination: hübsch, lobt, Siebs.

c. *Examples from vocal literature*

Ich ha*b* in *P*enna einen Lie*b*sten wohnen.

(*Ich hab in Penna;* Heyse, Wolf)

Ihr wallenden flis*p*ernden *P*a*pp*eln.

(*Der Jüngling an der Quelle;* Stoll, Schubert)

3. [d]

a. *Description*   [d] is the voiced alveolar stop, the English sound of the letter *d.*

b. *Spellings*

d before a vowel or *r* in the same syllable: dulden, andrehen.

dd: Kladde.

c. *Examples from vocal literature*

Denn *d*u, Hol*d*e, *d*enkst an ihn.

(*Botschaft;* Daumer, Brahms)

Stell auf *d*en Tisch *d*ie *d*uften*d*en Rese*d*en.

(*Allerseelen;* Gilm, Strauss)

4. [t]

a. *Description*   [t] is the voiceless alveolar stop, the customary sound of the letter *t* in English.

b. *Spellings*

t, tt: Titel, tragen, tut, Mutter, Bett.

th: Goethe, Noth.

d at the end of a word: Tod, Bad.

d at the end of a syllable: endlich, Handwerk.

d in a final consonant cluster: Stadt.

c. *Examples from vocal literature*

Wer rei*t*e*t* so spä*t* durch Nach*t* un*d* Win*d*?

(*Der Erlkönig;* Goethe, Schubert)

Das is*t* ein Flö*t*en un*d* Geigen, *T*rompe*t*en schme*tt*ern darein.

(*Das ist ein Flöten;* Heine, Schumann)

Aben*d*lüf*t*e im zar*t*en Laube flüs*t*ern.

(*Adelaide;* Matthisson, Beethoven)

5. [g]

a. *Description*   [g] is the voiced velar stop, the so-called "hard *g*" of English.

b. *Spellings*

g before a vowel in the same syllable: gegen.

---

[2] Fischer-Dieskau, however, pronounces *lieblich* with a voiced [b], which must therefore be considered an acceptable alternative.

g before *l, n,* or *r* in the same syllable: gleich, Gnade, greis.
gg: Flagge.

c. *Examples from vocal literature*
Wie *G*locken*g*eläute, durch *G*assen und Platz.

(Der Schmied; Uhland, Brahms)

Mor*g*enlicht leuchtend im rosi*g*en Schein.

(Die Meistersinger; Wagner)

6. [k]

a. *Description* [k] is the voiceless velar stop, the sound of the *k* and of the "hard *c*" in English.

b. *Spellings*

ch in some words of Greek derivation: Chor, Christ.

ch before *s:* Sachs, wechseln (unless the *s* is an inflective ending, as in *des Dachs*).

ck: Blick, decken.

k, kk: Kind, Kunkel.

q: Qual, erquicken.

g at the end of a word or syllable, or in a final consonant cluster, except after *i* or *n:* Tag, täglich, legst.

c. *Examples from vocal literature*
Den lieben We*g* zum *K*inderland.

(O wüsst ich doch; Groth, Brahms)

Hoch in den *K*ronen wogend sich's re*g*t.

(Aufenthalt; Rellstab, Schubert)

Auf ein Totena*ck*er hat mich mein We*g* gebracht.

(Das Wirtshaus; Müller, Schubert)

7. In addition to these six stops which are also found in English and which are represented by certain letters in spelling, the glottal stop (phonetic symbol [ʔ]) is also very common in German. It is used to begin words that start with a written vowel, unless there is very close connection with the preceding word. This sound is occasionally heard in English, most typically before each vowel in the familiar expression "oh-oh!" In German singing it is used less frequently than in conversational speech and should be reserved for cases where clear separation or strong emphasis is needed. For example, in the phrase "dein schmelzend Ach" in Brahms's *An die Nachtigall* the last two words need the clear separation afforded by a glottal stop to clarify the fact that the "Ach" is in a sense a quotation. In the phrase "meine eigne Gestalt," at the climax of Schubert's *Der Doppelgänger,* the introduction of the second word by a glottal stop imparts much dramatic strength.

B. NASALS

1. [m]

a. *Description* [m] is the labial nasal, the sound of *m* in English.

    b. *Spellings*

    m, mm: Mime, Sommer.

    c. *Examples from vocal literature*

    A*m* schwarzen Ka*m*in, da sitzet *m*ein Lieber.

(Der Schmied; Uhland, Brahms)

    Da niemand tröstet *m*ilden *M*under die ka*m*pf*m*üde Seele.

(Cäcilie; Hart, Strauss)

2. [n]

    a. *Description*   [n], the alveolar nasal, is the English pronunciation of the letter *n*.

    b. *Spellings*

    n except before a velar stop in the same syllable: nein.

    nn: Nonne.

    c. *Examples from vocal literature*

    O Schö*n*ste der Schö*n*en, be*n*imm mir dies Seh*n*en.

(O liebliche Wangen; Flemming, Brahms)

    *N*immer kommt ihr, Wo*nn*estu*n*den.

(Die Zauberflöte; Schikaneder, Mozart)

3. [ŋ]

    a. *Description*   [ŋ] is a velar nasal, often used in English as the sound of *n* before [k] (uncle) or [g] (finger) or as the sound of the whole combination *ng* (singing).

    b. *Spellings*

    n before [k]: denken, sank.

    Exception: The *n* and the *k* are in separate syllables when the *n* is the end of a prefix, as in *einkehren* [aenkerən], or the end of the first part of a compound word, as in *Rosenkranz* [rozən-krants].

    ng: Finger,[3] singen.

    Exception: The *n* and the *g* are in separate syllables when the *n* is the end of a prefix, as in *ungeduld* [UngədUlt], or the end of the first part of a compound word, as in *Schwanengesang* [ʃvanəngəsaŋ].

C. FRICATIVES

1. [v]

    a. *Description*   [v] is the voiced labio-dental fricative, corresponding to the English pronunciation of the letter *v*.

    b. *Spellings*

    v in a few foreign words: Vase, Klavier, Sklave.

    w: Wagner, ewig, Wonne.

    u after *q:* Qual, erquicken.

---

[3] Note that this is pronounced [fɪŋər], not [fɪŋgə] as in English. The pronunciation [ŋg], so common in English, is used in German only in a few foreign words.

c. *Examples from vocal literature*
Winterstürme wichen den Wonnemond . . .
Wunder webend er sich wiegt.

(*Die Walküre;* Wagner)

Querfeldein, durch Qualm und Schwüle.

(*Der Feuerreiter;* Mörike, Wolf)

2. [f]

a. *Description*   [f] is the voiceless labio-dental fricative, the sound of the letter *f* in English.

b. *Spellings*
f, ff: Fafner, Schiff.
v except in some foreign words: von, wieviel.
ph: Philosoph.

c. *Examples from vocal literature*
Tut sie dann, vielleicht, die Frage.

(*Botschaft;* Daumer, Brahms)

Was höchstem Lust verlangen Erfüllung kühn verhiess.

(*Die Meistersinger;* Wagner)

Ach, ich fühl's, est ist verschwunden.

(*Die Zauberflöte;* Schikaneder, Mozart)

3. [z]

a. *Description*   [z], the voiced alveolar fricative, corresponds to the usual sound of the letter *z* in English, and to the frequent pronunciation of *s* between vowels (rose, easy).

b. *Spelling*
s before a vowel: so, unser, langsam, dieser, Hänsel.
Exception: s at the end of the first part of a compound word, as in the Brahms song *In Waldeseinsamkeit* where the second word of the title, as well as the first word of the second line, *Windesatmen,* are compound words in which the *s* at the end of the first part of each is treated as a final *s* and is therefore voiceless.

c. *Examples from vocal literature*
Ich sehe mich gesund.

(*Dein blaues Auge;* Groth, Brahms)

Der Männer Sippe sass hier im Saal.

(*Die Walküre;* Wagner)

4. [s]

a. *Description*   [s] is the voiceless alveolar fricative and is the usual English pronunciation of *s, ss,* and "soft *c.*"

b. *Spellings*
s final: Hans, dies, als.
s before a consonant (except *p* or *t* at the beginning of a stressed *ss* (ß): Kuss, wissen.
syllable): ist, Sklave, lispeln, Röslein.

c. *Examples from vocal literature*
Wenn du es wüsstest, was träumen heisst.

(*Cäcilie;* Hart, Strauss)

Es ist unbekanntes Wehe.

(*Verborgenheit;* Mörike, Wolf)

5. [ʃ]

a. *Description* [ʃ] is a voiceless alveolo-palatal fricative corresponding to the sound of the combination *sh* in English. The voiced equivalent [ʒ] is found in German only in a few French borrowings, such as *Journal*. [ʃ] is pronounced in German with more lip-rounding than in English.

b. *Spellings*
sch: Schubert, hübsch, Esche.

Exception: On very rare occasions the *s* and the *ch* may be in separate syllables and should be pronounced independently. Such is the case in the opening phrase of Mahler's *Urlicht,* where *Röschen* is pronounced [røsçən] because the *s* is the end of the stem and the *ch* is the beginning of the suffix.

s before *p* or *t* at the beginning of a word or syllable: spät, Stadt, Wanderstab, Gespräch.

In case of doubt whether the *s* and the *p* or *t* are part of the same syllable, the placing of the stress is a fairly reliable guide. In general, where the letters are in combination at the beginning of the same syllable, the following syllable will bear either primary stress (*Gestalt*) or at least secondary stress (*Beispiele*); but where they are in separate syllables, the preceding syllable will be stressed, and the following absolutely unstressed (*gestern, lispeln*). In these latter cases, the *s* is pronounced [s] as the end of a syllable.

c. *Examples from vocal literature*
Der Nebel stieg, das Wasser schwoll.

(*Am Meer;* Heine, Schubert)

Gar schöne Spiele spiel ich mit dir.

(*Der Erlkönig;* Goethe, Schubert)

Am frisch geschnittnen Wanderstab.

(*Fussreise;* Mörike, Wolf)

6. [j]

a. *Description* [j] is the symbol used for the consonant in *yes, you, union* in English. In English, however, this is a palatal glide; that is, the vowel [i] is shortened so as to become a consonant. In German it is a voiced palatal fricative because the tongue approaches the palate a little more closely and moves away more sharply than in English so that a slight sound of friction is heard.

b. *Spelling*
j: ja, jeder, jetzt.

c. *Examples from vocal literature*
Liebst du um *J*ugend, o nicht mich liebe . . .
Liebst du um Liebe, o *ja*, mich liebe!
(*Liebst du um Schönheit;* Rückert, Mahler)
*J*auchzend grüsst sich das *j*unge Paar.
(*Die Walküre;* Wagner)

7. [ç]
a. *Description* [ç] is a voiceless palatal fricative. It can be made by putting the top of the tongue close to the palate in the position for the vowel [i], then expelling the breath very sharply between the tongue and the palate so that a sound like a cat's hissing results. This should be clearly distinguished from the consonant [ʃ] by the fact that the point of approximation between the tongue and the palate is a little farther back and by the fact that the lips are spread rather than round.

b. *Spellings*
ch after a front or a rounded front vowel: i*ch*, bre*ch*e, Bü*ch*er, eu*ch*, Rei*ch*.
ch after a consonant: Mäd*ch*en, Gret*ch*en.
g after *i* at the end of a word or syllable: ruhi*g*, Seli*g*keit.
Exception: When the suffix *lich* or the suffix *reich* follows, euphony demands the pronunciation [k] for the *g* in order to avoid the juxtaposition of two [ç] sounds.

c. *Examples from vocal literature*
Wehe, Lüft*ch*en, lind und liebli*ch*.
(*Botschaft;* Daumer, Brahms)
Und ziehe seli*g* mit dur*ch* ew'ge Räume.
(*Feldeinsamkeit;* Allmers, Brahms)
Meine Tö*ch*ter führen den nä*ch*tli*ch*en Reihn.
(*Erlkönig;* Goethe, Schubert)

8. [x]
a. *Description* [x] is a voiceless velar fricative. (A voiced velar fricative exists in some parts of Germany but is not recognized as standard German for stage and song.) It is pronounced by moving the back of the tongue up toward the soft palate so that the air passing between them causes a sound of friction. Contrary to some opinions, this is not a "guttural" sound and is not related to clearing the throat.

b. *Spelling*
ch after *a, o, u,* or *au:* Ba*ch*, do*ch*, ho*ch*, Bu*ch*, rau*ch*en.

c. *Examples from vocal literature*
O warum su*ch*t' ich na*ch* dem Glück?
(*O wüsst ich doch;* Groth, Brahms)
Ho*ch* glühn von den Wonneschauern der Na*ch*t.
(*Ständchen;* Schack, Strauss)

d. *Summary of* [ç] *and* [x] In a sense, these two voiceless fricatives are functions of the same sound, especially inasmuch as they are both spelled *ch*. Whether the hard palate or the soft palate is used to make the sound depends upon which is nearer to reach from the preceding vowel or consonant. If the tongue is in the front of the mouth for a consonant or a front vowel, [ç] is more convenient; if the tongue has just articulated a back vowel, [x] is more natural. In any case, the extremes of [ʃ] and [k] are to be carefully avoided. Also to be avoided is the intervention of other fricatives between [x] and [t] in words like *Nacht*. This word is occasionally pronounced by students something like [naxçʃst] because the tongue moves too slowly from one consonant to the other and picks up the intervening fricatives en route.

9. [h]

a. *Description* [h] is a voiceless laryngeal fricative and corresponds to the usual sound of *h* in English.

b. *Spelling* *h* except in two circumstances:

(1) *h* is silent following a vowel in the same syllable: Kuh, ihr, gehen. When *h* appears between two vowels, it is sometimes difficult to determine which vowel it goes with. In general, it goes with whichever vowel receives the stress. For example, *höher* has the stress on the first syllable and is pronounced [høər], but *woher* has the stress on the second syllable and is [voher]. It is presumed here, as in section 5b above, that singers will be able to infer the placing of the stress from the rhythm of the musical setting.

(2) Following *c, p, sc,* and *t,* the *h* is used to form a new sound. Note that *sh,* a common combination in English, is not a combination in German but two separate sounds. Pronounce the *s* and the *h* separately in words like *Wirtshaus* and *Aeolsharfe*.

c. *Examples from vocal literature*
Meine Ruh is *h*in, mein *H*erz is schwer.
(*Gretchen am Spinnrade;* Goethe, Schubert)
Wo*h*in, sprich, wo*h*in? Du *h*ast mit deinem Rauschen.
(*Wohin;* Müller, Schubert)
Ich sitze am Fenster und schaue *h*inaus in die Dunkel*h*eit.
(*Schlechtes Wetter;* Heine, Strauss)

D. AFFRICATES

German uses only two affricates, both voiceless.

1. [pf]

a. *Description* The combination [p] and [f] is treated in German not as two separate sounds, as in the English word *campfire,* but as a single combined sound, a voiceless labio-dental affricate.

b. *Spelling*
    pf: Pferd, Kopf.
c. *Examples from vocal literature*
    Mein Liedchen wegzu*pf*eifen . . .
    Der stum*pf*e Bursche bläht sich.
    (*Der Musensohn;* Goethe, Schubert)
2. [ts]
    a. *Description* Again, the combination of the two sounds [t] and
    [s] is treated in German not as two separate sounds, as in the
    English word *gets,* but as a single voiceless alveolar affricate.
    b. *Spellings*
        z: Mozart.
        zz: Skizze.
        c before a front vowel: Cäcilie.
        tz: Netz.
        t before *i* and another vowel: Nation, Patient.
    c. *Examples from vocal literature*
        Der Zeiten Wandel nicht zu seh'n, zum zweiten Mal ein Kind.
        (*O wüsst ich doch;* Groth, Brahms)
        . . . stolzes Herz, und jetzo bist du elend.
        (*Der Atlas;* Heine, Schubert)

E. LIQUIDS

1. [l]
    a. *Description* This is the sound of *l* and *ll* in English. When *l*
    follows a vowel in English, however, it is usually pronounced
    with the back of the tongue. While singers should avoid this pro-
    nunciation as much as possible because it tends to cause the pre-
    ceding vowel to sound swallowed, it is especially important to
    avoid it in foreign languages. The *l* following a vowel in German
    should be articulated with the tip of the tongue just like the *l*
    preceding a vowel.
    b. *Spelling*
        l, ll: lernen, als, Fall.
    c. *Examples from vocal literature*
        Geuss nicht so *l*aut die *l*iebentf*l*ammten Lieder, tonreichen Scha*ll*.
        (*An die Nachtigall;* Hölty, Brahms)
        In mi*l*dem *L*ichte *L*euchtet der *L*enz
        Auf *l*inden *L*üften, *l*ind und *l*ieb*l*ich.
        (*Die Walküre;* Wagner)
2. [r]
    a. *Description* The *r* in German should be flipped off the tip of
    the tongue in the manner of the British treatment of the *r* in such
    English words as *very, forest.* A double *r* is rolled slightly.
    Whereas in English we tend to suppress the *r,* especially the

flipped *r*, after a vowel, in German all *r*'s are treated identically whether before a vowel, after a vowel, or between two vowels. The only possible exception is the *r* after *e* at the end of an unstressed syllable (Winter, Vater), where German singers often omit the *r* if the note is very short and quite unimportant metrically. Note also that although, in German as in French, conversational speech often employs the uvular *r*, this *r* is never used formally.

b. *Spelling*
   r, rr: Rohr, Herr.

c. *Examples from vocal literature*
   *R*ufen d*r*aus vo*r* meine*r* Tür.

   (*Immer leiser wird mein Schlummer;* Lingg, Brahms)
   Mein a*r*me*r* Sinn ist mi*r* ze*r*stückt.

   (*Gretchen am Spinnrade;* Goethe, Schubert)

F. GLIDE

A glide is a vowel articulated very briefly and sharply so as to become a consonant. The only glide that can be identified in German is [ĭ], which is the vowel [ɪ] used as a consonant. This corresponds very closely to the pronunciation of the consonant [j] in such English words as *yes, un*ion; however, a different symbol is used in German to distinguish this sound from that of the voiced palatal fricative. Actually, the distinction is very slight indeed and consists only in the fact that the tongue is a little closer to the palate for [j] and moves away a little more abruptly so that a very slight sound of friction is heard. The voiced palatal glide [ĭ] is heard in German as the pronunciation of an *i* before another vowel in the ending *ion* (Nation, Vision) and before *e* in unstressed syllables where the *e* is pronounced [ə] (Lilie, Familie).[4]

---

[4] Cf. Chapter I, Part II, section A-1-b, and section D.

Chapter III

ALPHABETIC REVIEW OF GERMAN PHONETICS

a, aa, and *ah* are pronounced [a].
ä and *äh* are pronounced [ɛ].
ae and *aeh* are pronounced [ɛ].
ai is pronounced [ae].
au is pronounced [ao].
äu is pronounced [ɔø].
ay is pronounced [ae].
b is normally pronounced [b].
b at the end of a word or syllable is pronounced [p].
bb is pronounced [b].
c before a front vowel is pronounced [ts].
c before a consonant or a back vowel is pronounced [k].
ch after a front vowel or consonant is pronounced [ç].
ch after a back vowel is pronounced [x].
ch in some words of Greek derivation is pronounced [k].
chs is pronounced [ks].
ck is pronounced [k].
d is normally pronounced [d].
d at the end of a word or syllable is pronounced [t].
dd is pronounced [d].
e in absolutely unstressed syllables when final or when preceding *l, m, n, r, s, t,* or various combinations of these, is pronounced [ə].
e in the prefixes *ge* and *be* is pronounced [ə];

OTHERWISE

e before CC [1] is normally pronounced [ɛ],
    and
e final, before CV or before C/, is normally pronounced [e].
ee and *eh* are pronounced [e].

---

[1] In this summary the abbreviation CC will be used to stand for a doubled consonant or a consonant cluster, the abbreviation CV stand for a consonant followed by a vowel, and the abbreviation C/ to stand for a final consonant. Note again the exceptions given in Chapter I, Part I, especially in sections A-7, B-2, and B-3.

ei is pronounced [ae].

eu is pronounced [ɔø].

ey is pronounced [ae].

f and *ff* are pronounced [f].

g is normally pronounced [g].

g at the end of a word or syllable is pronounced [k], except after *i* or *n*.

g final after *i* is pronounced [ç].

gg is pronounced [g].

h is pronounced [h], except after a vowel in the same syllable or in the combinations *ch, sch, ph,* or *th.*

i before CC is normally pronounced [ɪ].

i final or before CV is normally pronounced [i].

i before C/ is normally pronounced [i].

i before C/ in some monosyllables and in unstressed suffixes is pronounced [ɪ].

ie and *ieh* are normally pronounced [i].

ie in some absolutely unstressed syllables is pronounced [ĭə].

ih is pronounced [i].

j is pronounced [j].

k and *kk* are pronounced [k].

l and *ll* are pronounced [l].

m and *mm* are pronounced [m].

n and *nn* are pronounced [n].

n before *k* in the same syllable is pronounced [ŋ].

ng in the same syllable is pronounced [ŋ].

o before CC is normally pronounced [ɔ].

o final, before CV or before C/, is normally pronounced [o].

ö (*oe*) before CC is normally pronounced [œ].

ö (*oe*) before CV or C/ is normally pronounced [ø].

oh and *oo* are pronounced [o].

öh is pronounced [ø].

p and *pp* are pronounced [p].

ph is pronounced [f].

qu is pronounced [kv].

r and *rr* are pronounced [r].

s before a vowel in the same syllable is pronounced [z].

s before most consonants is pronounced [s].

s at the end of a word or syllable is pronounced [s].

sch is pronounced [ʃ].

sp at the beginning of a word or syllable is pronounced [ʃp].

ss (ß) is pronounced [s].

st at the beginning of a word or syllable is pronounced [ʃt].

t and *tt* are pronounced [t].

ti before a vowel is pronounced [tsĭ].

tz is pronounced [ts].

u before CC is normally pronounced [ʊ].
u final before CV or before C/ is pronounced [u].
ü (*ue*) before CC is normally pronounced [ʏ].
ü (*ue*) before CV or C/ is normally pronounced [y].
uh is pronounced [u].
üh is pronounced [y].
v is normally pronounced [f].
v in foreign borrowings is often pronounced [v].
w is pronounced [v].
x is pronounced [ks].
y before CC is normally pronounced [ʏ].
y before CV or C/ is normally pronounced [y].
z and *zz* are pronounced [ts].

Chapter IV

FRENCH CONSONANTS

I. CONSONANTS IN DETAIL

A. STOPS

1. [b]
   a. *Description* The voiced labial stop is pronounced in French like the *b* of German and English.
   b. *Spellings*
      b, bb: bébé, abbé, bras.
   c. *Examples from vocal literature*
      Tournez, tournez, *b*ons chevaux de *b*ois.

      (*Chevaux de bois;* Verlaine, Debussy)

      L'om*b*re des ar*b*res dans la rivière em*b*rumée.

      (*L'Ombre des arbres;* Verlaine, Debussy)

2. [p]
   a. *Description* [p] is the voiceless labial stop and corresponds to the English *p*. Note, however, that the slight aspiration which follows all the voiceless stops in English and German should be suppressed in French, as in other Romance languages. That is, no expulsion of air should accompany the articulation of these consonants in French.
   b. *Spellings*
      p, pp: appel, père, lampe.
      Occasionally *b,* by assimilation with the voiceless quality of an *s* or a *t* following: absent, obstiné, obtenir.
   c. *Examples from vocal literature*
      Mais n'a*pp*ortant de *p*assion *p*rofonde.

      (*Au bord de l'eau;* Prudhomme, Fauré)

      Il n'est *p*lus de *p*arfum dans le *p*âle oranger.

      (*Les Roses d'Ispahan;* Leconte de Lisle, Fauré)

      Femme, qui *p*leures-tu?—L'a*b*sent!

      (*L'Absent;* Hugo, Fauré)

3. [d]
   a. *Description* The voiced alveolar stop corresponds to the *d* as

used in English, except that the placing of the tongue is just behind the upper teeth at the front rather than at the back of the alveolar ridge, as it is in English and German.

b. *Spellings*

d, dd: dindon, addition, descendre.

c. *Examples from vocal literature*

Une o*d*eur *d*ivine en ton sein.

(Lydia; Leconte de Lisle, Fauré)

*D*ans ce vague *d*'un *d*imanche.

(L'Echelonnement des haies; Verlaine, Debussy)

4. [t]

a. *Description* [t], the voiceless alveolar stop, differs from its English equivalent in two ways: (1) the tongue, as for [d], touches the front instead of the back of the alveolar ridge; and (2) there is no accompanying aspiration. These effects should be carefully practiced for a convincing French [t].

b. *Spellings*

t, tt: tête, attendre, triste.

th: théâtre, mythe.

c. *Examples from vocal literature*

*T*u m'appelais, et je qui*t*ais la *t*erre.

(Après un rêve; Bussine, Fauré)

*T*ou*t* au*t*our de *t*oi, vi*t*e, vi*t*e.

(Carmen; Bizet)

5. [g]

a. *Description* [g], the voiced velar stop, is the sound of the "hard *g*" in English.

b. *Spellings*

g or *gg* before *a, o, u,* or a consonant: gaz, gout, aigu, aggrégat.

gu before *e, i,* or *y:* figue, guise, Guy.

The first of two *g*'s before *e, i,* or *y:* suggérer.

c. *Examples from vocal literature*

Parmi les va*g*ues lan*g*ueurs.

(En sourdine; Verlaine; (1) Fauré, (2) Debussy)

Si c'est un *g*rand seigneur . . .

Il avait bonne *g*râce, a ce qu'il m'a semblé.

(Faust; Gounod)

6. [k]

a. *Description* The voiceless velar stop is like the English *k* except that, as for the other voiceless stops, the aspiration customary in English must be suppressed.

b. *Spellings*

c or *cc* before *a, o,* or *u,* or a consonant: Cannes, cor, occuper, clair.

c final: roc.

qu: quel, pique.

q final: coq.

k: kiosque.

The first of two *c*'s before *e, i,* or *y:* ac*c*ent, suc*c*ès.

ch in some words of Greek derivation, which may be recognized by their similarity to English cognates in which the *ch* is also pronounced [k]: Christ, écho, chœur.

   c. *Examples from vocal literature*

Et *q*ue les hommes *c*urieux.

(Les Berceaux; Prudhomme, Fauré)

Deli*c*atement, les *c*loches tintaient . . .

Dans le ciel *c*lément.

Rhythmi*q*ue et fervent *c*omme une antienne . . .

Me remémorait la blancheur *ch*rétienne.

(Les Cloches; Bourget, Debussy)

B. NASALS

  1. [m]

    a. *Description*   The labial nasal is the pronunciation of the English *m*.

    b. *Spellings*

m before a vowel: mer, imiter, âme.

mm: femme, comment.

    c. *Examples from vocal literature*

Je t'ai*m*e et *m*eurs, ô *m*es a*m*ours,

*M*on â*m*e en baisers *m*'est ravie.

(Lydia; Leconte de Lisle, Fauré)

*M*eurt co*mm*e de la fu*m*ée.

(L'Ombre des arbres; Verlaine, Debussy)

  2. [n]

    a. *Description*   This is the sound of the English *n*.

    b. *Spellings*

n before a vowel: nid, scène.

nn: anneau, Cannes.

    c. *Examples from vocal literature*

Quel trouble inco*nn*u me pé*n*ètre? . . .

La presence d'u*n*e âme i*n*nocente et divi*n*e.

(Faust; Gounod)

  3. [ɲ]

    a. *Description*   [ɲ] is a palatal nasal which does not occur in English or German but does occur in other Romance languages. The sound is very much like that of *ni* in the English word *onion* or of the *n* before [u] in such English words as *new, annual.* However, whereas the corresponding English sound is two consonants, [nj], the French sound is a single consonant made with a single gesture of the tongue. That is, whereas to form [nj] the tongue must move first to the alveolar ridge and then to the palate; to form [ɲ] it moves directly to the palate at the same time the nasal passages are opened.

b. *Spelling*
   gn: agneau, régner, digne.

c. *Examples from vocal literature*
   Donc, pour me tenir compagnie.

(Carmen; Bizet)

Mes frères craignent son courroux.

(Samson et Dalila; Saint-Saëns)

C. FRICATIVES

1. [v]

   a. *Description*   [v], the voiced labio-dental fricative, is pronounced like the English *v.*

   b. *Spellings*
      v: vivre, rêve.
      w when it occurs: wagon-lit.

   c. *Examples from vocal literature*
      L'amour vainqueur et la vie opportune.

(Clair de lune; Verlaine; (1) Fauré, (2) Debussy)

   Il vient, s'en va, plus il revient.

(Carmen; Bizet)

2. [f]

   a. *Description*   [f] is the voiceless labio-dental fricative, corresponding to the English pronunciation of the letter *f.*

   b. *Spellings*
      f, ff: faux, effet, chef.
      ph: philosophe.

   c. *Examples from vocal literature*
      Voici des fruits, des fleurs, des feuilles et des branches.

(Green; Verlaine; (1) Fauré, (2) Debussy)

   Ont fini par faire un infâme.

(Carmen; Bizet)

   Où flotte avec un chant plaintif l'ombre d'un if.

(Lamento; Gautier, Duparc)
(Au cimetière; Berlioz)

3. [z]

   a. *Description*   The voiced alveolar fricative corresponds to the usual English pronunciation of the letter *z.*

   b. *Spellings*
      s between two vowels, whether within the same word or in *liaison* (see Part III of this chapter): rose, mes amis.

z: zèle, azur.

c. *Examples from vocal literature*
J'ai des galants à la douzaine.

(*Carmen;* Bizet)
Ah! je suis heureuse!

(*Louise;* Charpentier)

4. [s]

a. *Description*   [s], the voiceless alveolar fricative, is the sound of the "soft *c*" and the frequent sound of *s* in English.

b. *Spellings*
s initial: sous, style.
s before or after a consonant: espérer, absent.
s final when pronounced (not in liaison, but pronounced in the original form of the word): hélas, Saint-Saëns, lys.
ss: laisser, classe.
c before *e, i,* or *y:* ce, ici, cygne.
ç: façon, reçu.
t before *i* followed by another vowel in such endings as *tie, tion, tient:* démocratie, nation, patient.

c. *Examples from vocal literature*
Tous deux, s'il glisse un nuage en l'espace.

(*Au bord de l'eau;* Prùdhomme, Fauré)
Un lys cache répand sans cesse.

(*Lydia;* Leconte de Lisle, Fauré)
C'est étonnant comme ça vous soûle.

(*Chevaux de bois;* Verlaine, Debussy)

5. [ʒ]

a. *Description*   [ʒ], the voiced alveolo-palatal fricative, is the sound of the medial consonant in the English words *vision, measure, azure.*

b. *Spellings*
j: je, jaune.
g before *e, i,* or *y:* loge, givre, gymnase.
ge or *je* before another vowel: nageais, Jean.
The second of two *g*'s before *e, i,* or *y:* suggérer.

c. *Examples from vocal literature*
Je rêvais le bonheur, ardent mirage.

(*Après un rêve;* Bussine, Fauré)
Toujours, toujours la protéger.

(*Faust;* Gounod)

6. [ʃ]

a. *Description*   [ʃ], the voiceless alveolo-palatal fricative, is the usual pronunciation of *sh* in English.

b. *Spelling*
ch: cher, toucher, vache.

c. *Examples from vocal literature*
Et dépê*ch*ez, *ch*evaux de leur âme.

(*Chevaux de bois;* Verlaine, Debussy)
Samson, re*ch*er*ch*ant ma présence.

(*Samson et Dalila;* Saint-Saëns)

7. [h]

It is customary to distinguish between two treatments of the letter *h* in French, the "mute *h*" and the "aspirate *h*." Both are normally silent; but the mute *h* prevents liaison and the elision of the vowel of the definite article (*l'heure,* but *la haine; l'homme* but *le héros*). Dictionaries normally show this distinction in some manner. French singers and actors often pronounce an aspirate *h* as [h] in words of strong emotional connotations, such as the word *haine* (hatred) and its related forms. Otherwise, the voiceless laryngeal fricative [h] does not exist in French.

D. LIQUIDS

1. [l]

a. *Description*   As in German, be sure to form the [l] with the tip of the tongue, even when it stands after a vowel; resist the normal English articulation which uses the back of the tongue after a vowel.

b. *Spellings*
l, ll: loup, bal, aller.

c. *Examples from vocal literature*
Appe*ll*e un chant p*l*aintif, éterne*l* et *l*ointain.

(*Aurore;* Silvestre, Fauré)
O b*l*anche Léïlah! que ton souff*l*e *l*éger.

(*Les Roses d'Ispahan;* Leconte de Lisle, Fauré)

2. [r]

a. *Description*   Even though the *r* is pronounced with a flip of the uvula in conversational French, especially in Paris and its environs, the flip of the tip of the tongue that characterizes the *r* of Italian and of British English is always used by French singers and actors in any formal context. English-speaking singers should remember that in French, as in German, *r*'s are not silent before consonants as they so often are in English.

b. *Spellings*
r, rr: raie, cher, narrer.

c. *Examples from vocal literature*
Comme un ciel eclairé pa*r* l'au*r*o*r*e.

(*Après un rêve;* Bussine, Fauré)
J'a*rr*ive, tout couve*r*t enco*r*e de *r*osée.

(*Green;* Verlaine; (1) Fauré, (2) Debussy)

II. FINAL CONSONANTS

There is an old rule-of-thumb stating that the only final consonants that are pronounced in French are the four in the English word *careful*. While it is true that final consonants are silent more often than not in French, the pattern is somewhat more complex, as we shall see. To begin with, there is one peculiarity that involves several different consonants: this concerns the numerals 5–10 (cinq, six, sept, huit, neuf, dix). When these numerals are used in counting, or otherwise in isolation, the final consonants are pronounced. However, when they are followed by a noun, either immediately (cinq jours, six mois) or with intervening modifiers (sept jolies femmes, dix jeunes filles), the final consonants are silent. Moreover, although *cinq, sept, huit,* and *neuf* have their final consonants pronounced regularly as [k], [t], [t], and [f] respectively when they are pronounced, *six* and *dix* have the irregular pronunciation [s] for the final *x* in circumstances when it is pronounced.

It should be further noted that, since the addition of a final *s* alters the pronunciation of a French word only very rarely, a consonant preceding a final *s* is treated for all practical purposes as a final consonant.

A. These consonants may be regarded as being normally pronounced when final:

c: lac, sec, avec, échec, roc.

> *Exceptions:* When final *c* follows *n,* it is usually silent (banc, tronc). However, the final *c* in *donc* is often pronounced for emphasis; and the name of the composer Poulenc has the final *c* pronounced. Other common exceptions (although not very common in vocal music) are *caoutchouc, porc,* and *tabac.*

f: chef, if, œuf.

> *Exceptions:* cerf, clef, nerf, chef-d'œuvre, œufs, bœufs. For the treatment of the numeral *neuf,* see above.

l: bal, bel, fil, fol.

> *Exceptions:* When final *l* is preceded by *i* preceded by another vowel, the *i* and *l* together are pronounced [j]. When *fils* means "threads" (as it does, for example, in the phrase "trame de fils d'argent" from Fauré's *Aurore*), it is pronounced [fil], just like *fil.* However, when *fils* means "son," as it much more often does, it is pronounced [fis]. Other common exceptions are *gentil, pouls,* and *saoul.*

q: coq. For the treatment of the numeral *cinq,* see above.

r: car, hiver, professeur, pur, tour.

> *Exceptions:* There are many words ending in *er* that have a silent final *r.* Two groups of words in particular may be distinguished:
> 1. First conjugation infinitives: aller, donner, parler.
> 2. Nouns, including many ending in *-er* and all ending in *-ier,*

which have connotations of occupations or functions, such as *boulanger* (baker), *épicier* (grocer), and *pommier* (apple-tree). Note, however, that many such words (professeur, voyageur) end in *eur* and have the final *r* pronounced. Singers who are in doubt whether a word ending in -*er* belongs to one of these categories should consult a dictionary, since words not belonging to one of these groups, such as *hiver* (winter), *cher* (dear), or *cuiller* (spoon), normally have the final *r* pronounced.

Words ending in *r* followed by another consonant or consonants most often have the *r* pronounced, the other consonants being silent: cerf, corps, mort, porc, lourd, vers.

B. These consonants may be regarded as being normally silent when final:

b: plomb.

d: fard, fond, pied, poids.

  Exceptions: sud and some proper names such as *Alfred.*

g: poing, sang.

m: daim, parfum.

  Exceptions: some Latin words, such as *album, maximum.*

n: fin, main, son.

p: camp, coup, drap, galop.

  Exception: cap.

s: bas, champs, corps, mais, pays, sous, and all inflective forms.

  Exceptions: There are a number of proper names, such as *Reims* and *Saint-Saëns,* which have a pronounced final *s.* There are, in addition, a number of other words in which a final *s* is pronounced. Most common among these are *bis, fils* (meaning "son"), *helas, jadis, lys* (or *lis* meaning "lily"; but the final *s* of *fleur-de-lis* is silent), *mars, mœurs, ours,* and *sens.* Moreover, there are several words that have different treatment of the final *s* according to usage and meaning. The noun *os* has the final *s* pronounced in the singular but silent in the plural. *Tous* as an adjective has the final *s* silent (tous les hommes sont partis: "all the men have left"); but when it is a pronoun, the final *s* is pronounced ("Moi, seule entre tous": "I alone of all"). *Plus* has the final *s* silent in its usual meaning of "more"; but when it means "plus," the final *s* is pronounced, as it is also in the phrase *en plus.*

t: lent, tôt, mort.

  Exceptions: dot, net, soit (as an adverb meaning "so be it"). For the treatment of the numerals *sept* and *huit,* see page 36. There are a number of possible final combinations involving *t;* several different pronunciations occur:

ct: sometimes both silent, as in *aspect;* sometimes both pronounced, as in *direct, exact, strict.*

gt: both silent, as in *doigt, vingt.*

lt: both silent, as in *Perrault.*

pt: both generally silent, as in *rompt* (but see the note about *sept* above).

st: sometimes both silent, as in *est* (is), *Jésus-Christ;* sometimes both pronounced, as in *est* (east), *ouest, Christ.*

x: deux, choix, toux, voix.

Exception: index, in which the final *x* is pronounced [ks]. For the treatment of the numerals *six* and *dix,* see page 36, and note that the final *x* when pronounced in these words is pronounced [s].

z: allez, chez.

Exceptions: Some proper names have a pronounced final *z.* In *Berlioz,* the final *z* is pronounced [z]; in *Austerlitz* and *Biarritz,* it is pronounced [ts]; in *Metz* it is pronounced [s].

III. LIAISON

A. Narrowly defined, *liaison* is the pronounciation of a normally silent final consonant before a word beginning with a vowel or with a mute *h.* Some authors use the term to refer to the use of any final consonant, but the issue becomes much clearer if the definition is limited to the sounding of consonants that would normally be silent.

Before any word beginning with a vowel or mute *h,* a normally silent final consonant may theoretically be pronounced. In practice, however, there are various limitations to its use. In conversational usage, liaison is limited to combinations that are closely connected grammatically. Passy [1] cites the following instances in which liaison is used in "la langue parlée":

1. Article followed by an adjective or a noun: les hommes, les autres personnes.
2. Adjective followed by a noun: le grand ours, deux petits enfants, mon ami.
3. Numeral followed by an adjective or a noun: deux animaux.
4. Adverb followed by an adjective or an adverb: tres utile, trop idiot.
5. Personal pronoun (or *en*) followed by a verb: il entend, nous arrivons, on ecoute, j'en ai.
6. Verb followed by a personal pronoun (or by *en, y*): a-t-il peur, vas-y, prends-en.
7. Preposition followed by its complement: sans abri, en écoutant.

[1] Paul Passy, *Abrégé de prononciation française* (Leipzig: O. R. Reisland, 1897), p. 13.

8. The conjunction *quand* and following words: quand il viendra.
9. Various forms of the verbs *être* and *avoir,* especially when used as auxiliaries, and following words: il est ici, il était arrivé, ils ont appris.

B. Liaison is used less sparingly in formal French. Some authorities [2] recognize several different levels of speech in which the declamation of verse uses the most numerous liaisons. When to make liaison is in fact one of the most intricate problems facing the non-French singer, since the sure knowledge of this requires a development of the ear and a discrimination that is possible only through years of careful listening. Unfortunately, *Phonetic Readings of Songs and Arias,* so helpful in most respects, is of little assistance in this matter, since liaison is given only where it would be used in casual conversation and thus is omitted in many places where French singers habitually make it. [3] The inexperienced singer should cultivate his taste for liaison by careful listening to recordings of French singers and actors. Meanwhile, he may do well to follow the advice of Sten, who says, "In poetic declamation . . . all possible liaisons are made," but cautiously follows this statement with some discussion of the meaning of the word "possible." [4] There are some cases in which liaison is never possible. Here are some:

1. Liaison should of course not be made when there is a clear syntactical separation, whether or not it is indicated by a breath or even by punctuation:
   "à te détester, / à me dire . . ."
2. Liaison is not made before a word beginning with an aspirate *h,* and singers should be careful to inform themselves from reliable dictionaries about such words:
   "sans amour et sans / haine . . ."
   "tournez au son des / hautbois . . ."
3. Liaison should not be made with the final *t* of the conjunction *et:*
   un homme et / une femme.
4. Liaison is usually avoided after a final *t* preceded by *r:*
   "dort / un clair de lune . . ."
   ". . . couvert / encore de rosée . . ."
   "cela ne sert / à rien . . ."
   "De chaque branche part / une voix . . ."
5. Liaison is not normally made with a final *m* or after a noun ending with *n* or *nt:*

---

[2] Cf. esp. Pierre Fouché, *Traité de prononciation française* (Paris: Librairie C. Klincksieck, 1959), pp. 437ff., and H. Sten, *Manuel de phonétique française* (Copenhagen: Ejnar Munksgaard, 1956), pp. 62ff.

[3] One of the most satisfactory treatments in English of this vexing problem is to be found in Chapter II of Part II of G. G. Nicholson's *Practical Introduction to French Phonetics* (London: Macmillan and Company, 1909).

[4] Sten, *op. cit.,* p. 65.

Le parfum / impérissable.

"Qui me rafraichissait le front / avec des palmes,

"Et dont l'unique soin / était d'approfondir . . ."

C. The pronunciation of a few consonants is altered in liaison:

d is carried as [t]: "Il m'apprend [t] à jouer . . ."

f in *neuf* is carried as [v]: neuf [v] heures.

g is carried as [k]: "Qu'un sang [k] impur . . ."

s and *x* are carried as [z]: mes [z] amis, beaux [z] yeux.

Chapter V

FRENCH VOWELS

A. FRONT VOWELS

1. [i]

a. *Description* [i], the highest front vowel, corresponds to the pronunciation of *e* in the English word *see* except that it is shorter than this vowel usually is in English and is articulated with more tension in the tip of the tongue.

b. *Spellings*

i: [1] ici, qui, midi.

î: île.

ie at the end of a word or syllable: [2] philosophie, reniement.

y: Debussy, Guy, lys.

c. *Examples from vocal literature*

Pui*s*que l'aube grand*i*t, pui*s*que voic*i* l'aurore.

(La bonne chanson; Verlaine, Fauré)

Lu*i*re dans son n*i*d, t*i*ssé d'herbes f*i*nes.

(Le Colibri; Leconte de Lisle, Chausson)

Grain de musc qu*i* g*i*s inv*i*s*i*ble.

(Hymne; Baudelaire, Fauré)

2. [e]

a. *Description* [e], as in German, is a sound which does not exist in its pure form in stressed syllables in English except as English is spoken in Ireland, Scotland, and the western plains of the United States. It is the vowel found in unstressed form in words like *chaotic* and *fatality;* but the moment these vowels become stressed (chaos, fatal), most English speakers add an off-glide toward [ɪ] or even [i]. This off-glide must by all means be avoided in French.

b. *Spellings*

ai final, especially in verb forms: gai, j'ai, j'irai, j'allai.

---

[1] Note that here and in all rules given for vowels it is to be assumed that the vowel is not preceded or followed by another vowel unless a combination is given.

[2] French syllables normally end with a vowel unless there is a doubled consonant or a consonant cluster, in which case the syllable divides between consonants.

e before a final silent consonant except *s* and usually *t:* régner, aller, chez, clef.

é: été, blé, vérité, éléphant.

Irregularly in the words *et* [e] and *pays* [pei].

c. *Examples from vocal literature*

Je me noir*ai* dans ta clart*é*.

(*Chanson triste;* Lahor, Duparc)

Souffr*ez* que ma fatigue à vos pi*eds* repos*ée*.

(*Green;* Verlaine; (1) Fauré, (2) Debussy)

Et dépêch*ez*, chevaux de leur âme.

(*Chevaux de bois;* Verlaine, Debussy)

3. [ɛ]

a. *Description*   [ɛ], as in German, must be clearly distinguished from [e]. It is the sound of the "short *e*" in such English words as *set, head.*

b. *Spellings*

è: cède, père, fidèle.

ê: fête, rêve, forêt.

e before a pronounced final consonant: bec, éternel.

e before two or more consonants: cesser, perdre.

Exception: If there is a syllable division before rather than between the consonants, the *e* is pronounced [ə]. Such is the case in many words beginning with the prefix *re* (reprendre, ressemble), some words beginning with *dess* (dessous, dessus), and a few other words (secret).

ai: laisser, aime, clair.

aî: maître.

aie: paie, raie.

aient in verb endings: allaient, auraient.

ei: peine.

ey: Beyle, Peyre.

e before final silent *t* (except in the monosyllable *et*): jet, est.

es in monosyllables: ces, des, les, mes, ses, tes.[3]

c. *Examples from vocal literature*

Qu*e*ll*e est* c*e*tte langueur qui pén*è*tre mon cœur?

(*Il pleure dans mon cœur;* Verlaine, Debussy)

R*ê*ve d*es* ch*e*rs instants.

(*Green;* Verlaine; Fauré, Debussy)

J*e* l*es* car*e*ss*ais,* et c'*é*t*aient* l*es* miens.

(*La Chevelure;* Loüys, Debussy)

4. [a]

a. *Description*   [a] is a vowel which is not normally found in

---

[3] The [e] vowel is normally used for these words in conversational French, but most French singers and actors use [ɛ]. Cf. Charles Bruneau, *Manuel de phonétique pratique* (Paris: Editions Berger-Levrault, n.d.), p. 81.

American speech. It is used in its short form in Great Britain and New England as a substitute for "short *a*" [æ] in words like *half, laugh, ask, bath, can't,* and the like (though many such speakers broaden this *a* all the way to the [ɑ] of *father*); and in its long form as a substitute for the diphthong [aɪ] in the speech of the southern United States. It is midway between [æ] (the "short *a*" prevalent in English) and [ɑ], from which it should be distinguished in French.

b. *Spellings*

a, à: la, là, car, papa.

i after *o:* doigt, moi.

Occasionally *e* before *mm* or *nn:* emmener, femme, solennel.

c. *Examples from vocal literature*

P*a*r to*i* conduit, ô main où trembler*a* m*a* main.

(*La bonne chanson;* Verlaine, Fauré)

L*a* c*a*r*a*v*a*ne humaine au S*a*h*a*r*a* du monde.

(*La Caravane;* Gautier, Chausson)

B. ROUNDED FRONT VOWELS

1. [y]

a. *Description* As in German, the vowel [y] is [i] pronounced with very much rounded lips; that is, the lips are in the position for [u] while the tongue is in the position for [i]. Again, as in German, the tongue position is more important than the lip position; and the substitution of [i], while incorrect, would be less objectionable than the substitution of [u] so frequently heard from English-speaking students. It is of course of the utmost importance that the lips be fully rounded before leaving the consonant preceding this or any other rounded vowel.

b. *Spellings*

u, û: du, dû, fut, murmure.

eu in parts of the verb *avoir:* eu, eut, eusse.

ue at the end of a word or syllable: revue.

c. *Examples from vocal literature*

Ô le frêle et frais m*u*rm*u*re, cela gazouille et s*u*s*u*rre.

(*C'est l'extase;* Verlaine; (1) Fauré, (2) Debussy)

D'*u*ne vapeur s*u*rnat*u*relle.

(*Romance;* Bourget, Debussy)

2. [ø]

a. *Description* [ø] is the vowel [e] pronounced with the lip-rounding of the vowel [o].

b. *Spellings*

eu or *œu* as the final sound in a word: dieu, heureux, nœud.

eu before [z]: creuse, Greuze, heureuse.

eû: jeûne.

c. *Examples from vocal literature*
Reviens, radi*eu*se, reviens, o nuit mystéri*eu*se!

(Après un rêve; Bussine, Fauré)

Mi*eu*x que le vent joy*eu*x.

(Les Roses d'Ispahan; Leconte de Lisle, Fauré)

Faîtes-lui mes av*eu*x, portez mes v*œu*x.

(Faust; Gounod)

3. [œ]

a. *Description*   [œ] is [ɛ] pronounced with the lips in the position of [ɔ].

b. *Spellings*

eu or *œu* in any position other than those described above: jeune, cœur, meunier.

ue after *c* or *g:* cercueil, orgueil.

œ in *œil*.

c. *Examples from vocal literature*
Il pl*eu*re dans mon c*œu*r.

(Il pleure dans mon cœur; Verlaine, Debussy)

Toute s*eu*le j'ai p*eu*r.

(Carmen; Bizet)

4. [ə]

a. *Description*   Unlike the neutral vowel in English, the schwa is pronounced with lip-rounding in French so that in singing it should sound about midway between [ø] and [œ]. It is the only French vowel which is absolutely unstressed.

b. *Spellings*   The letter *e* in these circumstances:

(1) In most cases where *e* would be silent in spoken French:

Final *e* except when followed by a word beginning with a vowel or mute *h:* aime, belle.

Except in monosyllables, before final *s:* aimes, belles.

In third person plural verb endings before final *nt:*[4] aiment, parlent, viennent.

In any case in which one of the above combinations directly follows a vowel, the *e* may be silent, as it is in spoken French. If the composer provides a separate note for the *e,* it should be sung as [ə]; if there is no separate note for it, it should be omitted. Furthermore, at any time when the *e* which is silent in spoken French is sung on the same note as the preceding syllable, it should be pronounced very unobtrusively, if at all.

(2) In these combinations where [ə] is also used in spoken French:

---

[4] Note, however, that there are many French words ending in *ent* which are not third person plural verb forms (différent, souvent, etc.). In case of doubt, consult a dictionary; if the word is not listed separately, assume it is part of a verb.

Final *e* in a monosyllable: ce, de, que.

e before any consonant directly followed by a vowel (that is, *e* which is final in a syllable): m*e*ner, gouvern*e*ment.

ai in these parts of the verb *faire:* faisons, faisant, f*ai*sais, f*ai*sait, faisions, faisiez, f*ai*saient.

c. *Examples from vocal literature*
S*e* plaign*ent* les tourt*e*rell*es*.

(*L'Ombre des arbres;* Verla·ne, Debussy)
Vos chèr*es* mains fur*ent* mes guid*es*.

(*La bonne chanson;* Verlaine, Fauré)
Sent*ent* leur mass*es* r*e*tenu*es*.

(*Les Berceaux;* Prudhomme, Fauré)

C. BACK VOWELS

As in German, all the back vowels are pronounced with lip-rounding except [ɑ]. Again, the lips must be fully rounded before the vowel sound is begun.

1. [u]
   a. *Description* [u] corresponds to the *oo* of such English words as *cool, moon,* except that there is even more tension in the lip-rounding of the French vowel than of the Engl:sh.
   b. *Spellings*
   ou, oû, où: boule, joujou, goût, où.
   oue at the end of a word or syllable: moue, dénouement.
   c. *Examples from vocal literature*
   Le r*ou*lis s*ou*rd des caill*ou*x.

(*C'est l'extase;* Verlaine; (1) Fauré, (2) Debussy)
T*ou*rnez cent t*ou*rs, tournez mille t*ou*rs,
T*ou*rnez s*ou*vent et t*ou*rnez t*ou*jours.

(*Chevaux de bois;* Verlaine, Debussy)

2. [o]
   a. *Description* [o] is the vowel found in unstressed syllables in such English words as *follow, obey.* Any suggestion of the off-glide which usually follows this vowel when it occurs in stressed syllables in English must be carefully avoided in French.
   b. *Spellings*
   o as the final sound in a word: argot, clos, galop.
   o before [z]: chose, rosier.
   ô: aumône, rôle.
   Exception: hôtel [ɔtɛl].
   au, eau: beau, bureau, haut, saule.
   c. *Examples from vocal literature*
   L'une à la ch*o*se et l'*au*tre à la p*o*se.

(*Chevaux de bois;* Verlaine, Debussy)

Vois sur ces can*aux* dormir ces vaiss*eaux*.

(*L'Invitation au voyage;* Baudelaire, Duparc)

Qui part tr*op* tôt revient tr*op* tard.

(*Bonjour Suzon;* Musset, Delibes)

3. [ɔ]

a. *Description*   [ɔ] corresponds to the vowel found in such English words as *cause, for, walk*, except that, whereas the English vowel is always long, the French vowel is usually short. For this reason the latter strikes the English ear as sounding much like the vowel [ʌ] used in English in such words as *flood, love, mud.* The only distinction, in fact, between [ʌ] and the short [ɔ] used in French is that the former is not pronounced with lip-rounding as the latter is. Thus, such French words as *bonne* and *mode* sound like the English words *bun* and *mud* pronounced with slight lip-rounding.

b. *Spellings*

o in any position except those listed above: bonne, homme, monotone, soleil.

au before *r:* Fauré, mauresque.

In some Latin words, *u* before final *m:* album, maximum.

c. *Examples from vocal literature*

B*o*nne f*o*ret! Pr*o*messe ouverte de l'exil que la vie impl*o*re.

(*Dans la forêt de Septembre;* Mendès, Fauré)

Voix de n*o*tre desespoir, le r*o*ssign*o*l chantera.

(*En sourdine;* Verlaine; (1) Fauré, (2) Debussy)

La n*o*te d'*o*r que fait entendre le c*o*r.

(*La bonne chanson;* Verlaine, Fauré)

4. [ɑ]

a. *Description*   [ɑ] corresponds to the "broad *a*" (*calm, father*) of English. The spellings for this sound are much like those for [a], and in many instances the singer will have to check a reliable dictionary for the exact pronunciation. On the other hand, as was pointed out in section C-5 of the second part of Chapter I, the distinctions in sound between [a] and [ɑ] are likely to be less marked in singing than in speech.

b. *Spellings*

â: âme, fâcher, grâce, pâle.

a before [s] occasionally when it is spelled *c*, more often when it is spelled *ss:* espace, classe, passer.

a before [z] occasionally when it is spelled *z*, more often when it is spelled *s:* gaz, emphase, occasion.

a before final silent *s:* pas, tas.

Exceptions: Second person singular endings in the future tense, such as *diras*, end in [a], as does the word *bras.*

i after *o,* especially before a final silent consonant: bois, froid, voix, poids, loi.

  c. *Examples from vocal literature*

    C'est l'ext*a*se langoureuse . . . c'est tous les frissons des bo*i*s
. . . le chœur des petites vo*i*x.

            (*C'est l'extase;* Verlaine; (1) Fauré, (2) Debussy)

    Parfo*i*s luisaient des b*a*s de jambes.

                    (*Les Ingénus;* Verlaine, Debussy)

D. NASAL VOWELS

In general, nasal vowels occur in French whenever an *n* or *m* is final or whenever *n* or *m* precedes another consonant other than another *n* or *m*. In such cases the *n* or *m* is not pronounced as a consonant but instead causes the preceding vowel to take on a nasal quality. A similar effect occurs in conversational English, especially in the United States, but only when the nasal precedes a voiceless consonant, as in such words as *jump, can't, think.* In nasalizing a vowel, care should be taken to cause some of the air to pass through the mouth. If all the exhaled breath comes through the nose, the resulting sound is unpleasant and unacceptable for singing. The French nasal vowels can be ugly, but the great French singers and actors have demonstrated repeatedly that they can also be extremely beautiful when they are pronounced with full resonance.

When a final *n* or *m* is carried in liaison (see Chapter V, final section), the preceding vowel remains essentially the same vowel, though it may lose some of its nasality. It does not, however, revert to the vowel that would be used before a different consonant. The addition of [⁓] over a phonetic symbol indicates nasality; otherwise the phonetic symbols are pronounced in the usual manner, except that [ɛ̃] is a little more open than [ɛ], and more like the English vowel [æ] ("short *a*"). In the rules that follow, always assume that the *n* or *m* is final or is followed by another consonant; if *n* or *m* is doubled or followed by a vowel, it is pronounced, and the preceding vowel is pronounced just as it would be before any other consonant.[5]

One further word of caution should be given with regard to all the nasal vowels. In words in which *m* precedes *b* or *p,* or in which *n* precedes *d* or *t,* special care must be taken not to sound the nasal consonant itself. If the *b, p, d,* or *t* is articulated before the nasal passages have been closed, an intervening *m* or *n* will be heard. This can be prevented by being sure that the release of the nasality and the articulation of the following consonant are absolutely simultaneous. The sounding of *m* before *b* or *p,* and of *n* before *d* or *t,* is one of the most

---

[5] Two exceptions that are common enough to be noted are *ennui* and *enivrer,* with all their inflections and derivatives, which are pronounced with [ɑ̃] in the first syllable.

common faults of English-speaking singers (and, even more conspicuously, of Italian singers) singing in French.[6]

1. [ɛ̃]
   a. *Description*   [ɛ̃], as noted above, has more the quality of the English "short *a*" (phonetic symbol [æ]) than that of the vowel [ɛ].
   b. *Spellings*
      aim, ain: daim, main, sainte.
      eim, ein: Reims, ceinture, hein.
      en after *i:* bien, chrétien, viens.
      im, in: imparfait, simple, cinq, loin, matin.
      ym, yn: symbole, symphonie, synthèse.
   c. *Examples from vocal literature*
      Appelle un chant pl*ain*tif, éternel, et lo*in*tain.
      (*Aurore;* Silvestre, Fauré)
      Rev*iens,* rev*iens,* ma b*ien*-aimée.
      Comme une fleur lo*in* du soleil.
      (*L'Absence;* Gautier, Berlioz)

2. [ã]
   a. *Description*   [ã] should be kept quite open so that it sounds distinct from both [ɑ] and [ɔ̃]. A most common fault among English-speaking students is making [ã] and [ɔ̃] sound identical because the former is not quite open enough and the latter not quite round enough.
   b. *Spellings*
      am, an: ample, jambe, bande, hanter.
      em, en (except after *i*): emphase, sembler, gens, tendre.
   c. *Examples from vocal literature*
      Un vaste et t*en*dre apaisem*ent* s*em*ble desc*en*dre du firmam*ent.*
      (*La bonne chanson;* Verlaine, Fauré)
      (*L'Heure exquise;* Hahn)
      Cep*en*dant l'excell*ent* docteur bolonais.
      (*Fantoches;* Verlaine, Debussy)
      Tout *en* ch*an*tant sur le mode mineur.
      (*Clair de lune;* Verlaine; Fauré, Debussy)

3. [ɔ̃]
   a. *Description*   [ɔ̃] is definitely rounder than [ã] and not so open.
   b. *Spellings*
      om, on: bombe, ombre, pompe, bon, honte, ronfler.
   c. *Examples from vocal literature*

---

[6] A most effective method for remedying this fault was recently suggested by the distinguished singer and teacher Norman Farrow, who advised students who find themselves sounding *m* before *b* or *p*, or *n* before *d* or *t*, to imagine a respelling of troublesome words so that *n* precedes *b* or *p* and *m* precedes *d* or *t*. Thus, the phrase "semble descendre" might be respelled "senble descemdre," since it is impossible to sound *n* before the *b* or to sound *m* before the *d*.

M*on* cœur craintif, m*on* s*om*bre cœur . . .
L'avenir dût-il m'être s*om*bre
Et féc*on*d en peines sans n*om*bre.

(*La bonne chanson;* Verlaine, Fauré)

4. [œ̃]

    a. *Description*   In the current Parisian speech this vowel is often abandoned in favor of the unrounded [ɛ̃]; this substitution should be avoided in formal French.

    b. *Spellings*
       um, un: humble, parfum, défunt, Verdun.

    c. *Example from vocal literature*
       N'est-il plus *un* parf*um* qui reste?

(*Romance;* Bourget, Debussy)

E. GLIDES

Functionally glides are consonants, but they are vowels used as consonants. The three glides are [j], [ɥ], and [w], and they are, respectively, the three vowels [i], [y], and [u] used as consonants. Whenever *i, u,* or *ou* appears in French before another vowel, the first vowel is shortened to the point of becoming a consonant and a glide results (bien, hier, lui, nuage, fouet, oui). There are two exceptions:

When the second vowel is *e* final or when it is *e* followed by final *s,* by final *nt* (third person plural verb ending), or by a single consonant followed directly by another vowel, the first vowel retains its regular vowel quality and the *e* is silent. Another way of expressing this is to state that wherever the conversion of *i, u,* or *ou* into a glide would result in the second vowel's becoming [ə], the first vowel is not converted to a glide but remains a pure vowel. The *e* may be silent or may be sung as [ə], depending upon whether the composer has provided a note for it. Here are some examples:

Final *e:* vie [vi], lue [ly], moue [mu].

e before final *s:* vies [vi], lues [ly], moues [mu].

e before final *ent* in the third person plural verb forms: rient [ri], tuent [ty], jouent [ʒu].[7]

e before CV: reniement [rənimɑ̃], dénouement [denumɑ̃].

Occasionally a composer will decide to provide a note for the first vowel. In such a case the singer has no choice but to sing the note on a pure vowel sound, since notes cannot be sung on glides any more than on any other consonants. For example, the word *radieuse* would normally be pronounced [radjøz]; but in *Après un rêve* Fauré has set the word syllabically on four notes, and it must be sung [radiøzə]. The word *silhouette* is spoken as [silwɛt]. However, Fauré in *La bonne*

---

[7] But note, as was pointed out in Chapter IV, section B-4, that the *ent* ending is not always a sign of the third person plural verb form. For example, *vient* is a third person singular form meaning "he comes" and is pronounced [vjɛ̃].

chanson and Hahn in *L'Heure exquise* both treat it as a four-syllable word, and it must be sung [siluɛtə]. Actually, this practice is not as arbitrary as it has been made to sound here but is directly related to the syllabification of the poetry.

1. [j]

    a. *Description* [j], the palatal glide, corresponds to the usual English pronunciation of *y* or *i* used as a consonant (yes, mill*i*on).

    b. *Spellings*

        i before another vowel (but note exceptions given above): bien, hier, science.

        il final when preceded by a vowel: deuil, émail, soleil.

        ille final preceded by a vowel: grenouille, travaille.

        ille final sometimes even when preceded by a consonant: fille, brille. BUT *ville* and *mille* and *tranquille* end in [il].

        ill preceded and followed by a vowel: cailloux, éveillai.

        ill followed by a vowel, sometimes when preceded by a consonant: brillant, fillette. BUT *village* and *million* have [il] in the first syllable.

    c. Note these peculiarities about the vowel sound preceding the *il* or *ill* pronounced [j]:

        (1) When no vowel precedes the *i*, the *i* does double duty, serving both as the principal vowel and palatalizing the *l*. Thus, *fille* is [fij], *brillant* is [brijɑ̃].

        (2) However, when another vowel precedes the *i*, it serves alone as the main vowel, neither combining with the *i* to form a new vowel nor converting to a glide. Thus, *cailloux* is not [kɛju], as it would be if the *a* and *i* combined to form [ɛ], but [kaju]; *grenouille* is not [grənwij] as it would be if the *ou* became a glide before *i*, but [grənuj]. In other words, the *i* combines with the *l* or *ll* to form a new sound, doing double duty as a vowel only when there is no other vowel in the syllable.

    d. *Examples from vocal literature*

        Les sole*il*s mou*ill*és de ces c*i*els brou*ill*és.

                (*L'Invitation au voyage;* Baudelaire, Duparc)

        C'est que la forêt v*i*e*ill*issante . . .

        De sa prem*i*ere feu*ill*e morte.

                (*Dans la forêt de Septembre;* Mendès, Fauré)

2. [ɥ]

    a. *Description* [ɥ] is the vowel [y] shortened to form a consonant. It is one of the most difficult of French sounds for English-speaking singers to master; and one often hears [w] erroneously substituted. The difference, like the difference between [y] and [u], lies in the tongue position. [ɥ] has the tongue position of [i], not that of [u]; [w] has the more retracted tongue position of [u].

Singers who have difficulty should practice from two different directions: (1) substitute [y], then gradually shorten the first vowel until it becomes a glide; thus, [lyi . . . lɥi] or [nyaʒ . . . nɥaʒ]; and (2) substitute [j], then round the lips over the [j] so that it becomes [ɥ]; thus, [lji . . . lɥi] or [njaʒ . . . nɥaʒ].

b. *Spelling*

u before another vowel (but note the exceptions given above):
juin, lui, nuage.

c. *Examples from vocal literature*

Pour un cœur qui s'ennuie, ô le bruit de le pluie!

(*Il pleure dans mon cœur;* Verlaine, Debussy)

Et du luisant buis je suis las.

(*Spleen;* Verlaine, Debussy)

3. [w]

a. *Description* [w] corresponds to the usual sound of *w* in English except that the lips are more prominently and more tensely rounded than is often the case in English.

b. *Spellings*

ou before a vowel (again, note the exceptions): fouet, Louis, oui.

o before *i:* joie, loin, mois.

c. *Example from vocal literature*

Oui, Dieu le veut! Je dois suivre ton ordre . . .

Pourquoi frémir? L'effroi remplit mon âme!

(*Jeanne d'Arc;* Tchaikovsky)

Chapter VI

ALPHABETIC REVIEW OF FRENCH PHONETICS

a is usually pronounced [a].

a before [s] or [z] is often pronounced [ɑ].

a before final silent *s* is usually pronounced [ɑ].

à is pronounced [a].

â is pronounced [ɑ].

ai is usually pronounced [ɛ].

ai final is usually pronounced [e].

ai in parts of *faire* (see Chapter IV, section B-4) is pronounced [ə].

aim and *ain* [1] are pronounced [ɛ̃].

am and *an* are pronounced [ɑ̃].

au is normally pronounced [o].

au before *r* is pronounced [ɔ].

b and *bb* are normally pronounced [b].

b before *s* or *t* is pronounced [p].

c and *cc* before *a, o, u,* or a consonant are pronounced [k].

c before *e, i,* or *y* is pronounced [s].

cc before *e, i,* or *y* is pronounced [ks].

ç is pronounced [s].

ch is normally pronounced [ʃ].

ch in a few words of Greek derivation is pronounced [k].

d and *dd* are normally pronounced [d].

d in liaison is pronounced [t].

e final is pronounced [ə] except before a vowel or a mute *h,* where it becomes silent.

e before CV is pronounced [ə].

e before CC is normally pronounced [ɛ].

e before CC is often pronounced [ə] in the *re* prefix.

e before a final pronounced consonant is pronounced [ɛ].

e before a final silent consonant (except *s* or *t*) is pronounced [e].

é is pronounced [e].

---

[1] Here and in all combinations ending in *m* or *n* that appear below, it is assumed that the *m* or *n* is final or that it is followed by another (different) consonant. Otherwise, of course, the nasal vowel does not obtain.

è and *ê* are pronounced [ɛ].

eau is pronounced [o].

ei is pronounced [ɛ].

eim and *ein* are pronounced [ɛ̃].

em and *en* are normally pronounced [ɑ̃].

en after *i* is pronounced [ɛ̃].

ent final in a third person plural verb ending is pronounced [ə].

es final is normally pronounced [ə].

es final in monosyllables is pronounced [ɛ].

et final is pronounced [ɛ] except in the monosyllable *et* (and), which is pronounced [e].

eu (*œu*) is normally pronounced [œ].

eu as a final sound is pronounced [ø].

eu before [z] is pronounced [ø].

eû is pronounced [ø].

ey is pronounced [ɛ].

f and *ff* are pronounced [f].

f in liaison is pronounced [v] in the word *neuf*.

g and *gg* before *a, o, u,* or a consonant are pronounced [g].

g before *e, i,* or *y* is pronounced [ʒ].

g in liaison is pronounced [k].

gg before *e, i,* or *y* is pronounced [gʒ].

ge before *a* or *o* is pronounced [ʒ].

gn is pronounced [ɲ].

gu before a vowel is pronounced [g].

h is normally silent, though an aspirate *h* may sometimes be pronounced [h] for a dramatic effect.

i before a consonant is pronounced [i].

i before a vowel is normally pronounced [j].

î is pronounced [i].

ie final is pronounced [i] or [iə] depending on the number of notes provided.

ie before CV is pronounced [i] or [iə].

ien is pronounced [jɛ̃].

ient (third person plural verb ending only) is pronounced [i] or [iə].

ies final is pronounced [i] or [iə].

il final after a vowel is pronounced [j].

ill between vowels is pronounced [j].

ill after a consonant, before a vowel is sometimes pronounced [ij], but sometimes [il].[2]

ille final after a vowel is pronounced [j].

ille final after a consonant is sometimes pronounced [ij], but sometimes [il].[3]

---

[2] *Ville, mille, tranquille,* and their derivatives are the only frequently encountered words in these groups in which the [il] pronunciation is used.

[3] *Ibid.*

im and *in* are pronounced [ɛ̃].

j is pronounced [ʒ].

k is pronounced [k].

l and *ll* are pronounced [l] except sometimes after *i* (see above).

m and *mm* are pronounced [m].

n and *nn* are pronounced [n].

o is normally pronounced [ɔ].

o as the final sound in a word is pronounced [o].

o before [z] is pronounced [o].

ô is pronounced [o].

oi is pronounced [wa] or [wɑ].

oin is pronounced [wɛ̃].

om and *on* are pronounced [ɔ̃].

ou before a consonant is pronounced [u].

oû and *où* are pronounced [u].

ou before a vowel is normally pronounced [w].

oue final is pronounced [u] or [uə], depending upon how many notes are provided.

oue before CV is pronounced [u] or [uə].

ouent final (third person plural verb ending) is pronounced [u] or [uə].

oues final is pronounced [u] or [uə].

p and *pp* are pronounced [p].

ph is pronounced [f].

qu and *q* final are pronounced [k].

r and *rr* are pronounced [r].

s is normally pronounced [s].

s between vowels and in liaison is pronounced [z].

ss is pronounced [s].

t is pronounced [t].

th is pronounced [t].

ti before a vowel in certain noun and adjective endings is pronounced [sj].

tie final is pronounced [si].

u before a consonant is pronounced [y].

û is pronounced [y].

u before a vowel is normally pronounced [ɥ].

ue final is pronounced [y] or [yə], depending upon the number of notes provided.

ue before CV is pronounced [y] or [yə].

ue after *c* or *g* is pronounced [œ].

uent (third person plural verb ending) is pronounced [y] or [yə].

ues final is pronounced [y] or [yə].

um and *un* are pronounced [œ̃].

v is pronounced [v].

w is usually pronounced [v].

x before a consonant is pronounced [ks].

x before a vowel is normally pronounced [gz], occasionally [ks].

x in liaison and in *deuxième, sixième,* and *dixième* is pronounced [z].

y after a consonant is pronounced [i].

y between two vowels is treated as *ii;* that is, the first hypothetical *i* combines with the preceding vowel and the second hypothetical *i* becomes [j]. Thus, rayon = *rai-ion,* therefore [rɛjɔ̃]; *soyez* = *soi-iez,* therefore [swaje]; *fuyons* = *fui-ions,* therefore [fɥijɔ̃].

ym and *yn* are pronounced [ɛ̃].

z is pronounced [z].

The diaeresis (··) is used in French to indicate some irregularity in vowel treatment, usually a separation of two vowels that would otherwise be combined into a single sound, as in *haïr* [air]; occasionally the alteration or omission of a vowel sound, as in *Saint-Saëns* [sɛ̃sɑ̃s].

Appendix I

REFERENCE LIST OF COMMON GERMAN PREFIXES AND PREPOSITIONS USED AS PREFIXES

Many aspects of the pronunciation of German depend upon whether or not certain letters belong to the same syllable. Since the syllable always divides after a prefix, it is most helpful for the student to be able to identify prefixes. Here, therefore, is a reference list of common German prefixes and prepositions used as prefixes:

ab	ent	um
an	er [1]	un
auf	für	unter
aus	ge	ver [3]
be	her [2]	voll
bei	hin	von
da	in	vor
dar	mit	wo
dort	nach	zer [4]
durch	ob	zu
ein	so	

[1] The *er* element in all these prefixes is pronounced [ɛr].
[2] *Ibid.*
[3] *Ibid.*
[4] *Ibid.*

Appendix II

SAMPLE TRANSCRIPTIONS OF GERMAN TEXTS

I. *Die Mainacht* (Hölty, Brahms)

Wann der silberne Mond durch die Gesträuche blinkt,
[van   der zɪlbərnə mont dʊrç di gəʃtrɔøçə blɪŋkt

Und sein schlummerndes Licht über den Rasen streut,
ʊnt zaen ʃlʊmərndəs   lɪçt ybər den rɑzən ʃtrɔøt

Und die Nachtigall flötet, wandl' ich traurig von Busch zu Busch.
ʊnt di naxtigal   fløtət vandl ɪç traorɪç vɔn bʊʃ tsu bʊʃ

Überhüllet vom Laub girret ein Taubenpaar
ybərhylət fɔm laop gɪrət aen taobənpar

Sein entzücken mir vor; aber ich wende mich,
zaen entsʏkən mir for abər ɪç vɛndə mɪç

Suche dunklere Schatten, und die einsame Träne rinnt.
zuxə dʊŋklərə ʃatən   ʊnt di aenzamə trɛnə rɪnt

Wann, o lächelndes Bild, welches wie Morgenrot
van   o lɛçəlndəs bɪlt vɛlçəs vi mɔrgənrot

Durch die Seele mir strahlt, find ich auf Erden dich?
dʊrç di zelə mir ʃtralt fɪnt ɪç aof erdən dɪç

Und die einsame Träne bebt mir heisser die Wang herab.
ʊnt di aenzamə trɛnə bept mir haesər di vaŋ hɛrap]

II. *O du mein holder Abendstern* (Wagner)

Wie Todesahnung Dämmrung deckt die Lande; umhüllt das Thal mit
[vi todəsˀanʊŋ   dɛmrʊŋ   dɛkt di landə   umhylt das tal   mɪt
schwärzlichem Gewande,
ʃvɛrtslɪçəm   gəvandə

Der Seele, die nach jenen Höh'n verlangt,
der zelə di nax jenən høn   fɛrlaŋt

Vor ihrem Flug durch Nacht und Grausen bangt.
for irəm fluk dʊrç naxt ʊnt graozən baŋt

57

Da scheinest du, o lieblichster der Sterne,
da ʃaenəst du o libliçstər   der ʃtɛrnə

Dein sanftes Licht entsendest du der Ferne,
daen zanftəs lɪçt   ɛntzɛndəst du der fɛrnə

Die nächt'ge Dämmrung theilt dein lieber Strahl,
di nɛçt gə dɛmruŋ   taelt   daen libər ʃtral

Und freundlich zeigst du den Weg aus dem Thal.
ʊnt frɔøntlɪç   tsaekst du den vek aos dem tal

O du mein holder Abendstern,
o du maen hɔldər ʔabəntʃtɛrn

Wohl grüsst' ich immer dich so gern;
vol grʏst ɪç imər dɪç zo gɛrn

Vom Herzen, das s'e nie verrieth,
fɔm hɛrtsən das zi ni fɛrit

Grüsse sie, wenn sie vorbei dir zieht,
grʏsə zi vɛn zi forbae dir tsit

Wenn sie entschwebt dem Thal der Erden,
ven zi ɛntʃvept   dem tal der erdən

Ein sel'ger Engel dort zu werden.
aen zelgər ɛŋəl dɔrt tsu verdən]

Appendix III

EXERCISES IN "ADJACENT" VOWEL SOUNDS IN FRENCH

The student is advised to read these series of words into a tape recorder, being careful to make the differences among the three words in each series distinct, but minimal:

Series A [i], [e], [ɛ]. These are all front vowels, the tongue position becoming progressively lower.

dit, dé, des

fit, fée, fait

Guy, gai, guet

gis, j'ai, j'aie

nid, né, nait

qui, quai, qu'est

Series B [i], [y], [u]. The vowel in the second word should have the tongue position for the first word and the lip position for the third word.

fit, fut, foux

gis, j'eus, joue

lit, lu, loup

nid, nu, nous

ci, su, sous

vie, vu, vous

Series C [e], [ø], [o]. Again, the vowel in the second word has the tongue position for the first word, the lip position for the third word.

bébé, bœufs, beau

dé, deux, dos

fée, feux, faux

j'ai, jeux, jaune

né, nœud, nos

Series D [ɛ], [œ], [ɔ]. Once more, the vowel in the second word has the tongue position for that in the first word, the lip position for that in the third word.

des, deuil, dort

fait, feuille, fort

l'air, leur, lors

maire, meurs, mort

net, neuf, note

sel, seul, sol

Series E [y], [ø], [œ]. These are all rounded front vowels, the tongue position becoming progressively lower.

du, deux, deuil

fut, feux, feuille

j'eus, jeux, jeune

nu, nœud, neuf

su, ceux, sœur

vu, veux, veuve

Series F   [u], [o], [ɔ]. All are back vowels, becoming progressively more open and less rounded.

doux, dos, dot   soux, Sceaux, sol
foux, faux, fol   nous, nos, note
moue, mot, mort

Series G   [ɛ̃], [ɑ̃], [ɔ̃]. These nasal vowels should be kept quite distinct, with the second lower than the first and the third somewhat rounded.

daim, dans, dont   nain, n'en, non
lin, lent, long   pain, pend, pont
main, ment, mon   sain, sans, son

Appendix IV

SAMPLE TRANSCRIPTIONS OF FRENCH TEXTS

I. *Chanson triste* (Lahor, Duparc)

Dans ton cœur dort un clair de lune, un doux clair de lune d'été,
[dɑ̃   tɔ̃   kœr   dɔ   rɑ̃̃   klɛr   də   lynə   ɑ̃̃   du   klɛr   de   lynə   dete

Et pour fuir la vie importune, je me noierai dans ta clarté.
e   pur   fɥir la vi   ɛ̃   pɔrtynə   ʒə   mə   nware   dɑ̃   ta   klarte

J'oublierai les   douleurs passées, mon amour; quand tu berceras
ʒu   blire   lɛ   du   lœr   pɑseə   mɔ   namur   kɑ̃   ty   bɛrsəra

Mon triste cœur et mes pensées dans le calme aimant de tes bras!
mɔ̃   tristə kœ re   mɛ   pɑseə   dɑ̃   lə kal   mɛ mɑ̃   də tɛ   bra

Tu prendras ma tête malade Oh! quelquefois sur tes genoux;
ty   prɑ̃ dra   ma tɛtə maladə o   kɛl kəfwa   syr tɛ ʒənu

Et lui diras une ballade qui semblera parler de nous,
e   lɥi dira zynə   baladə   ki   sɑ̃   bləra parle   də   nu

Et dans tes yeux pleins de tristesses, dans tes yeux alors je boirai
e   dɑ̃   tɛ zjø   plɛ̃   də tristɛsə   dɑ̃   tɛ zjø   zalɔr   ʒə bware

Tant de baisers et de tendresses que peut-être je guérirai.
tɑ̃   də bɛ ze ze də tɑ̃ drɛsə   kə   pøt trə   ʒə gerire]

II. *Micaëla's Air* (Bizet)

Je dis que rien ne m'épouvante, je dis, hélas, que je réponds de moi;
ʒə di kə   rjɛ̃   nə me puvɑ̃tə   ʒə di   elɑs   kə   ʒə repɔ̃   də mwa

Mais j'ai beau faire la vaillante, au fond du cœur je meurs d'effroi!
mɛ   ʒe bo   fɛrə la vajɑ̃tə   o fɔ̃   dy kœr   ʒə mœr   defrwa

Seule en ce lieu sauvage, toute seule j'ai peur, mais j'ai tort
sœl   ɑ̃ sə ljø sovaʒə   tutə   sœlə ʒe   pœr mɛ   je tɔr
    d'avoir peur;
    davwar pœr

Vous me donnerez du courage, Vous me protégerez, Seigneur!
vu   mə dɔnəre   dy kuraʒə   vu   mə prɔteʒəre   sɛɲœr

61

Je vais voir de près cette femme dont les artifices maudits
ʒə vɛ vwar də prɛ sɛtə famə dɔ̃ lɛ zartifisə modi

Ont fini par faire un infâme de celui que j'aimais jadis!
ɔ̃ fini par fɛ rœ nɛ̃famə də səlɥi kə ʒɛmɛ ʒadis

Elle est dangereuse, elle est belle, mais je ne veux pas avoir peur!
ɛl ɛ dɑ̃ʒərøzɛ ɛl ɛ bɛlə mɛ ʒə nə vø pɑ zavwar pœr

Non! Je parlerai haut devant elle. Ah!
nɔ̃ ʒə parləre o dəvɑ̃ tɛlə a

Seigneur, Vous me protégerez!
sɛɲœr vu mə prɔteʒəre]

Bibliography

Bruneau, Charles. *Manuel de phonétique pratique.* Paris: Editions Berger-Levrault, n.d.

Coffin, Berton, *et al. Phonetic Readings of Songs and Arias.* Boulder: Pruett Press, 1964.

Fouché, Pierre. *Traité de prononciation française.* Paris: Librairie C. Klincksieck, 1959.

Marshall, Madeleine. *The Singer's Manual of English Diction.* New York: G. Schirmer, 1946.

Martens, Carl and Peter. *Phonetik der deutschen Sprache.* Munich: Max Hueber Verlag, 1961.

Moulton, William G. *The Sounds of English and German.* Chicago: The University of Chicago Press, 1962.

Nicholson, G. G. *A Practical Introduction to French Phonetics.* London: Macmillan and Company, Ltd., 1909.

Nitze, Williams, and Wilkins, Ernest. *A Handbook of French Phonetics.* New York: Henry Holt and Company, 1918.

Passy, Paul. *Abrégé de prononciation française.* Leipzig: O. R. Reisland, 1897.

Siebs, Theodor. *Deutsche Hochsprache,* ed. Helmut de Boor and Paul Diels. Berlin: Walter de Gruyter and Company, 1956.

Sten, H. *Manuel de phonétique française.* Copenhagen: Ejnar Munksgaard, 1956.

Viëtor, Wilhelm. *German Pronunciation: Practice and Theory.* Leipzig: O. R. Reisland, 1913.